Introduction

CW01501338

Whatever a successful career means to you, a well-planned job search and a thoroughly prepared interview are the inevitable hurdles we have to clear to attain it. It may be that you measure success in terms of financial rewards, status or position. Others seek self-fulfilment through their work and worry little about status or money. Either way, the job that is right for you will enable you to be an achiever and become the most effective person you can be.

This book is intended to help all those facing the challenge of mounting a job search. It will show you how to go about looking for work, how to approach employers, how to prepare your c.v. and write letters of application. And, perhaps most important of all, it will help you to prepare yourself for the selection interview.

An interview can be a daunting experience, but with proper self-evaluation and preparation it need not be. Whether it is for a place at a college or on a training course, a first job for a school or college leaver, a different or better job, returning to work after a long gap, or even a complete career change, these interview tips will help you to present yourself and your skills in the most positive light. It will be particularly helpful for women who wish to return to work after a long interval, those who have never found a satisfactory career, the long-term unemployed, and those who have been made redundant, and who are now facing the job market again with diminished self-confidence, uncertainty and trepidation.

One of the most important things for your job search and the development of your interview technique is to recognize that skills can be transferred from one field (where you acquired them) to another. Once you have mastered the basic points about self-appraisal and writing applications you will dramatically increase your chances of getting an interview. Being aware of the kinds of questions you may be asked will help you to become one of those people who always interviews well. Follow the tips about confidence-boosting and creating the right impression and you will always feel you have the interview situation under your control. Job offers will follow.

People who are normally confident about being able to do a particular job well often appear weak when it comes to interviews. It is very easy to feel overawed by the stress and strangeness of the situation and to give in to a feeling of powerlessness. This is where careful and thoughtful preparation can help. If you know yourself well and have thought about your skills and attributes and set your goals for the future, you will never again be at a loss in an interview.

When you are selected for interview, you may be one out of five or ten who have been shortlisted from a number of applicants amounting to perhaps several dozen. The shortlisted interview candidates will be amongst the best in the field, but only one person can be selected. Job hunting has a high failure rate. Regretfully, the interviewer must turn down the others, all of whom may be excellent in their way (although there will probably be some who disqualify themselves straight away by being casual, uninformed, or unmotivated). For the rejected candidates, of course, a miss is as good as a mile. But in a large number of cases, the result of an interview will be a close-run thing. The tragic part is that it is all too often the very person who possesses all the right qualities, abilities, experience and know-how who fails to come across in an interview. Frequently, the person who is selected is not the best candidate, but someone who knows how to put themselves over positively at an interview. Perhaps this candidate is the more extrovert and creates a lively impression, but this does not necessarily reflect the qualities needed in the job. Indeed many jobs are task-oriented and do not call for particularly out-going types of people.

This book is written in the belief that getting an interviewer to offer you a job or a place at university is a skill, and a skill that can be learnt. As Dick Lathrop pointed out in a book called *Who's Hiring Who*, "the person who gets hired is not necessarily the one who can do that job best; but, the one who knows the most about how to get hired". This doesn't mean there's a

SETTING YOUR SIGHTS

SETTING YOUR SIGHTS

Chris Brightwell

An IKON Career Guide

First published in 1991
by IKON Productions Ltd

ISBN: 1 871805 00 7

IKON Productions Ltd
Oxford

Printed in Great Britain

CONTENTS

shortcut. There isn't one. In fact, getting a job depends upon a good deal of hard work, research, and preparation. It also demands discipline, self-knowledge and rigorous self-appraisal of one's personal qualities and motives.

The rewards will be great. Job satisfaction, good financial remuneration, and interesting prospects for the future are major factors in building self-esteem. Being in the right job means feeling good about yourself and your place in the world. To be in the wrong job — well, it's the square-peg-in-the-round-hole feeling which in the long run no hobby, outside interest, or even a full family life can ever quite assuage. Winning the right job for yourself is quite simply the best favour you can do for yourself — and for all those who may happen to share their lives with you.

There cannot be many times in one's life when one sets out on a journey without caring what the final destination is, or indeed whether one arrives anywhere at all. It is impossible to achieve unknown goals, to realize unspecified ambitions or to fulfil unrecognized dreams. But, curiously, this is something that people frequently attempt when it comes to their careers, taking jobs that will have far-reaching effects on their lives with little thought of the likely destination. This has been all too often the case with women, the majority of whom have tended to accept the uncompetitive, underpaid jobs leaving the more satisfying and better-paid work to men. Typically, too, women have taken up the caring professions, but not always at a high enough level to ensure long-term job satisfaction.

From time to time I have asked people how they came to be doing the jobs they're doing. I have often found that "fate", luck or chance has played a part and, for some, the outcome has been successful. But the other part of the question, "What would you really like to be doing?" is most revealing and the answers usually differ quite radically and surprisingly from the person's actual occupation.

Many people end up doing jobs they dislike because they have never given adequate thought to what they want out of life or how they can achieve it. Very few people are lucky enough to find themselves making a living from what they enjoy doing most. But work takes up such a large part of our lives that it seems only sensible to consider the rewards and satisfactions that it will bring and to try to mesh one's natural skills and abilities with the characteristics the job demands. *Setting your Sights* will help you to identify and target your career in accordance with the values and preferences dictated by your personality.

CHAPTER ONE

Trends in Recruitment in the 90s

One of the biggest changes seen in patterns of employment this century is that people are no longer born and brought up in tightly-knit communities where the eldest son is expected to follow his father's occupation. We have also seen the demise of traditional occupations and the rapid rise of new and challenging careers, unknown even a few years ago. Up until the 1980s the majority of workers were manual blue-collar workers, employed to perform manual skill-based tasks. Now that so much of our industry and manufacturing has been revolutionized by rapid changes in technology, this picture has changed. White collar jobs now outnumber manual ones — and will continue to dominate the employment market in the future. Information technology has blurred the edges between technical and general management roles. The shopfloor technician now has more information, decision-making power, and responsibility through information technology than his predecessors would have believed possible. As a consequence the power of decision-making has become decentralized, creating looser organizational structures.

In the external environment, technological development, scientific research, political upheaval, market forces and financial instruments are changing faster than ever before. Organizations need to tap all this knowledge in order to make informed choices about how they will change and develop. Those who want to compete will need to know how to respond to all this information and will require a more specialized workforce with a high level of knowledge and skill in dealing with information and its presentation. More training will be required to keep up with technological and economic developments. We have already seen many traditional jobs become redundant and, as this trend continues, there will be an increasing need for continuing education and training throughout a person's career. Varied opportunities are now demanded; role change will be regarded as the norm. The rapid rise in the rate of change calls for increased speed of response and adaptation to new developments. At present there is a marked shortfall between the skill base of the working population and the skills actually required, particularly in engineering, technology, health care, and secretarial work. However, even with a constant programme of re-training it is likely that the numbers of people capable of doing a particular job will dwindle. Organizations will thus seek to recruit and train their own workforces rather than rely upon external recruitment. With this kind of investment in staff, companies will have to try harder to keep their trained personnel. The parenting years will have to be made easier for staff with appropriate spans of parental leave, crèches, and regular up-dating courses so that those who decide to have children won't find their skills becoming obsolete and their careers languishing as a result.

The difficulty of finding adequately-trained staff will be exacerbated by the need for the service industries to supply services outside traditional working hours. This trend certainly applies to retailing, tourism, the leisure and catering industries and also to transport. Employees must therefore be flexible about their working hours and willing to adapt their skills to meet the needs of changing job functions. This increased flexibility is likely to lead to short- or fixed-term contracts and increased reliance upon freelance workers in place of the traditional employment contract with its provisions for job security. Competition from Eastern Europe and the Far East will place increased emphasis on holding down labour costs. One major result of this will be a dramatic shift towards payment for performance rather than time worked. This will be accompanied by a restructuring of companies. A small core of workers whose jobs are highly specific to that particular organization will be employed at enviable rates of remuneration, job security and career growth. Their knowledge and skills will be scarce and therefore highly valuable. Although they will only ever be a very tiny proportion of the workforce, they will be highly sought after by competing firms. Company re-training schemes will be focused upon these élite workers. This core of exceptionally well-qualified staff will be supported by employees — typists, receptionists, drivers or assembly workers — whose support is needed for the smooth running of the organization, but these support staff will possibly work part-time or share their jobs with others.

Part-time staff, agency workers, job-sharers, and sub-contractors will make up the balance of workers by providing skilled services on temporary or fixed-term contracts. The flexibility this method of working allows greatly favours the female workforce who may choose to work while bringing up a family, but who may wish to work only part-time or to have time at home with children during the holidays. Nearly three million people currently fall into this group of workers. More will be required. It has been estimated that by the end of the Nineties only half the working population will be in a full-time job. Organizations will wish to bring together teams of people to perform a particular task or complete a particular project and the team will be disbanded when the job is accomplished. These team workers will need to be flexible and adaptable, able to defer to the team leader who will be the person with the most skills and experience relevant to the job in hand, not necessarily the most senior person in the group. The European Community is currently pressing for these temporary and part-time workers to be assured of the same rights, perks, and benefits on a pro rata basis — holiday entitlement, sick pay and pensions, for example — as full-time employees.

Any company which fails to realize that its people are its greatest resource and asset is already doomed. Companies have paid lip-service to this idea for far too long. It is now necessary for there to be proper support and back-up for staff. This should include flexible working practices, continual training programmes so that those taking time out to have a family do not lose out on their long-term career goals, and a long-term attitude taken towards adequate leave for parenting needs. Staff who have been expensively trained will be more use to a company even after a family break than starting again with totally new staff.

In Britain the majority of women work; there are some 11.5 million women workers making up 40 per cent of the workforce. Two-thirds of all working women are married and six out of ten women at work in this country have a school-age child. Many women take up work in response to economic pressures as families often find it impossible to make ends meet unless both partners work.

But there are other factors. Women, even when sufficiently well off not to work, may prefer to, enjoying the independence, the satisfaction of earning for themselves, the challenge of pursuing a career, and the stimulus of interests, community and responsibilities outside the home. Increasingly, a partnership is becoming a voluntary companionship of two extremely busy individuals who have careers, interests and activities of their own. Women who enjoyed the freedom of the Sixties, with its opportunities for radical change, are now in their forties and enjoying managerial power in organizations or, indeed, in the running of their own enterprises. For these trend-setters and opinion-formers success at work is an important way of confirming their own identity independently of a spouse.

Work also provides a social context, offering people the opportunity of adult interaction; indeed many people's social lives revolve around their place of work. Social forecasters are fond of putting forward a scenario where most people work at home, connected to their work-base by means of a computer. This may be desirable for some, but the absence of regular personal contact with others is one of the major factors in depression, and so the social and community aspects of work should not be underestimated.

In 1959, the Crowther Report on education recommended that girls should be encouraged to consider courtship and marriage as central to their lives. Personal appearance and the problems of human relationships were to be the main focus of an adolescent girl's education. It has taken almost exactly thirty years for the government to take a contrary stance and to begin to encourage girls to prepare for careers with the same consideration for their long-term prospects as boys. Marriage itself has changed status; it is no longer seen as either a social necessity or a desirable goal. Of those who do marry, almost a third will be on their own again within a few years as marriage increasingly fails in the face of twentieth-century pressures. For those left on their own with children to raise by themselves, a rewarding and remunerative career is especially important. Single parents

14

in particular find they need to earn well to provide for their families.

Women now consider their careers much more than they did previously. It's important to have a real skill to market. Career decisions made early in life have long-term effects and women who find themselves frustrated and unable to progress at work are often feeling the results of not seeking proper training and qualifications early enough, or of allowing themselves to drift into dead-end jobs where there can be little expectation of promotion.

For many women returning to work after having had a family, there are similar frustrations. Perhaps this is the first time they have given any consideration to the skills necessary to finding a worthwhile job. Although it is never too late to learn new skills, it is undoubtedly easier when one is still young and has the energy and the time to spare.

In the past it has generally been the pattern for women to drift into work without giving enough thought to where they would like to be and what they would like to be doing in a few years' time. Perhaps it is only after she has already been at work for many years that a woman will be struck by the thought that she will be working day in day out for many years to come and must look to her future prospects. Only then does she start to look around for the means to acquire the skills and knowledge, help and training, which her brother thought about whilst still at school. One's choice of work is the first adult decision in life, often taken at school whilst preparing for examinations. It should be taken with forethought for the future, but many people take A-levels in the subjects they did best at O-level and only realize later on with some dismay that that decision has already determined the kind of jobs or further training for which they can apply.

Job satisfaction comes from feeling stretched, drawing on inner resources, using one's brain, ingenuity, imagination and wit. It comes, too, from having places to go, people to meet, things to do. The right sort of work can uncover one's potential in unexpected ways, resulting in the pleasure of taking one's place in the world, feeling useful and using one's talents and gifts. In short, work can be the making of you.

In this competitive market, however, recruitment will fall generally as the demand for full-time employees with a small range of skills to offer declines. Of those who have a high-level skill and specialized knowledge base — and perhaps languages — employers will seek a very precise match with their exact requirements. At the same time the pool of prospective employees will shrink due to increasing job specialization. There will be quite simply fewer people capable of doing the job in question at all. In fact, this trend has already begun. During late 1989 and early 1990, almost 25 per cent of companies needing to recruit 25 or more staff found themselves faced with significant difficulties of securing adequately-trained personnel. The ramifications bode ill for British businesses: recruitment difficulties put undue stress on existing staff and restrict business development. Turnover of permanent staff is likely to fall dramatically, but although the overall number of vacancies will be small, the task of attracting candidates and making a good match between them and the job will become more exacting. It is against this highly competitive job recruitment market that you will have to pit yourself and win, whether you want long-term job security or continuous flexible working. It is clear, however, that jobs offering long-term job security and the best rewards will demand a high degree of entrepreneurial skill as well as an understanding of policy and finance.

CHAPTER TWO

Choosing the Right Career

Work tends to be the dominating aspect of one's life for upwards of forty years. A career should be chosen with all the care and consideration normally reserved for a long-term partnership. It is good sense to consider your personality traits and to decide whether security is of paramount importance to you, — or travel, or meeting people, or working out of doors. Try to clear away prejudices. Some people feel, for example, that industry is boring, and yet industry offers many interesting careers especially if you are interested in management or if you have an entrepreneurial bent but do not want — at this stage at least — to go it alone. Prejudices are usually based on ignorance, so try to find out all you can about what sort of careers are available to you. Even within one field, there are many different jobs. A hospital career, for example, covers a wide range of varied occupations each with its own challenges and satisfactions: doctor, surgeon or consultant; physiotherapist; radiologist; midwife; administrator; nurse; counsellor; laboratory technician and so on.

What seems clear, however, is that irrespective of specific skills, there will be certain general expectations to be met in order to succeed in the 90s workplace. People will need to be at home with information technology, to have a wide general knowledge, which will probably include a reasonable depth of knowledge of at least one European country, market, and language, a flexible approach to work and the ability to work effectively with others in teams. They will need to be able to learn and keep on learning in order to keep up with a rate of change faster than any we have yet known. In addition there will be a premium to be paid in terms of salary and benefits for certain areas of work.

The 90s people most in demand will include designers, managers, scientists and engineers, computer people, and marketing and sales people who must be multi-lingual if they are to operate successfully in Europe. Well-qualified teachers, secretaries and health professionals will also be in demand. Unfortunately, there is likely to be a shortage of these people, because we already have a lack of adequately-trained people to teach them. Physics, a required subject for most engineering degrees, is a notable example. With such a lack of trained personnel, it is possible that Britain will have to draft in better qualified staff from abroad.

The Thatcher decade has been one of slimness for companies. The shedding of staff characteristic of the early 80s has resulted in lean companies aiming at high productivity and paying high salaries for work-driven Yuppies. Organizations have now been cut back to such a level that the only competitive advantage left is a drive for quality. With a lean workforce it is especially important to produce goods that are right first time. Valuable resources are squandered by having to put right mistakes that could have been avoided. This means investment in good design, reliable manufacture, and the proper monitoring of systems. Large corporates such as Ford, and Marks and Spencer have already begun a major drive towards ever higher quality standards and this will be a crucial factor in competing in European markets. Customers now expect a high level of service, too, which means companies will need to pay more attention to good customer relations.

It is not enough to have academic or technical expertise if you are not good with people. The emphasis on quality of service means that more employees will have to interface with clients, relate to their needs, find out about their problems and find ways of solving them. For example, a traditional accountancy firm may find that its staff are increasingly being asked for management consultancy for which accountancy qualifications are not strictly necessary. As this activity grows, it may come to dominate the business to such an extent that it is no longer necessary to recruit only qualified accountants. The firm will have changed its activities from offering a professional service to offering a commercial one. But to make the management consultancy side of the business profitable in a highly competitive area, it may be necessary to market it more aggressively, so the staff will have to be involved in marketing the service, attracting and securing new clients and managing new projects.

Rewards

Money is not everything and it is better to do something you enjoy than something you hate, no matter how well rewarded it is. However, it's no use pretending that money is not a major motivation in most people's lives. Your salary is going to determine where and how you live, what you do with your free time, where you spend your holidays and how you cope with fluctuating economic pressures, such as a sudden surge in interest rates. Good financial rewards will tide you over a bad patch at work, whereas, if you are poorly paid, this can be a perpetual source of worry.

Pay varies widely even where broadly similar skills are called for. Advertising is relatively well paid, Publishing relatively poorly paid, and yet the skills required are not so different as all that. Location makes a difference too. A competent secretary/PA in London will earn as much as a lecturer in a provincial university. The rewards of work do not necessarily reflect the type of work or its merits, so bear this in mind when deciding what kind of work you want to do. Also needs and wants vary throughout life. Young people entering employment for the first time may seek opportunities for travel, variety, early career growth and job interest. The more mature employee may well be strongly motivated by money in order to finance family responsibilities. Self-worth as reflected in job status and a high standard of living will also count for a good deal. The older person, however, whose children have grown up and left home, will have different values and may seek work that offers genuine job satisfaction and opportunities for self-realization.

Research on staff turnover suggests that a high salary does not always improve performance at work or encourage the retention of staff in the long run. Considerations of flexible working hours, a pleasant environment and quality of life may be just as important motivational factors. A good knowledge of what you want out of life will help you to negotiate your salary and other terms when the time comes. The traditional career structure that progresses steadily upwards in a strict hierarchy, bringing increased status and financial rewards on the way, may turn out not be the most satisfactory after all. The opportunity to develop new skills, and take on new challenges and experiences may

19

well prove more attractive to someone in youthful middle-age, eager to maximize their potential.

Will it last?

The industrial revolution of the 18th and 19th centuries came about through the mass production of manufactured goods for export to the British colonies which did not have the manufacturing capability to provide those goods for themselves. The latter part of the twentieth century has seen a dramatic change from the production of low value added goods to high value added goods, utilizing the newest technologies, for which high prices can be charged. As a result many jobs in manufacturing have declined in importance or even ceased altogether within the last couple of decades. The technology boom of recent years has destroyed many traditional fields of manually-skilled work. These jobs losses are not to be regretted. Some appallingly dull and arduous jobs in manufacturing have now been replaced by robots and wonders of automation and this sort of change is only to be welcomed.

Unfortunately, the teaching profession, long considered a secure and worthwhile career, has seen a marked decline in recent years owing to a variety of social and economic factors. Teachers of physics, maths, languages, and design are in particularly short supply and yet these are the very subjects likely to be most in demand from employers in the 90s. Recent manpower research indicates that organizations are already finding it difficult to recruit sufficient graduates in the fields of engineering, electronic and electrical engineering, science and technology, and computer studies. So we know there is a need for expertise in information technology, mechanical engineering, electrical engineering, physics and chemistry, accountancy, law, healthcare, teaching and design.

In our present phase of economic growth and intense competition, marketing and sales have come to the fore. The 80s have seen the steady growth of retail and service industries. Languages are certain to be in demand in the single European market. Traditional careers where people progress steadily up a ladder of promotion only to topple off into retirement at the end seem likely to be a thing of the past: people will be expected to change jobs repeatedly throughout their working life. Everyone will need to keep up with the new technology as it is developing. Individuals and companies must be committed to continual re-training as new techniques and technologies are perfected. Only by keeping your skills up to date will you be at the forefront of technological advances and be able to command a correspondingly high salary. The need for a constant retraining programme can be gauged by the fact that 75 per cent of the total working population of the year 2000 is already at work now.

Irrespective of subject specialization, the 90s will need certain types of people, people who are willing and able to learn and go on learning. The ability to acquire new skills and knowledge throughout their working life will ensure their continued demand. In addition there is likely to be continued employment for people who can work within changing structures. They must be able to work in teams, sometimes taking the lead themselves, and sometimes deferring to whomever on the team has the most experience for the particular task or project in hand. There will be new ambiguities in the work place as formalization drops away to be replaced by flexible units of people forming project teams and disbanding when the task is accomplished.

Planning ahead

If you have stayed on at school, or even gone to college or university, you may feel that you have earned the right to enjoy a good start, with a high salary and status reflecting your academic qualifications right from the word go. Most employers recognize that academic qualifications indicate that you have a good brain, a trained mind, and the ability to apply yourself to the job in hand. But even with all these advantages, there is still some way to go before you will be really useful to the company. Most of the very big corporates will want to train you in their way of doing things and recruitment will frequently be to a management trainee course.

New graduates are now finding themselves very much in demand for recruitment and this is likely to continue as graduates become scarcer owing to the declining birth-rate of the

1970s. Nine per cent of graduate jobs advertised in 1987 remained unfilled by the end of that year. Graduate entry salaries have risen by 18 per cent since 1982. Some firms have offered the "golden hello" of a lump sum payment to those they perceive as the brightest and best of students, though whether many can afford this practice which is so obviously open to abuse is doubtful. Employers will seek to attract new graduates by paying them well early on and by means of other perks too. However, it is likely — and to your long-term benefit — that you will need further training. The employer will need you to acquire particular business skills if you are to be of real value to the company. Indeed it is not unusual for a large company to treat this training as part of its selection procedure, taking on many more trainees than it will employ permanently.

When applying for jobs, choose those where you will be given a chance to learn and grow. Ultimately this is more important than a high status, highly-paid job straight away in a job where your career may stagnate. Building a career that will be satisfying and rewarding to you for most of your working life, does take time, energy and commitment. If you are prepared to learn new things constantly throughout your working life you will be a tremendous asset to your employer. It will also be a stimulus, keeping your mind alert, broadening your horizons and increasing your prospects.

Getting ahead

It's not always possible to arrive at a perfect match of attributes, but I believe the key to job satisfaction lies somewhere there, if only because it enables one to progress. A job in which one has little interest is a job that is hard to do well. Yet promotion generally depends upon just that. Only by doing a job well enough to have one's efforts recognized and rewarded by being given another better job can one escape the vicious circle of dissatisfaction at work. Without proper thought and planning a job can become, all too easily, a trap from which it is hard to plot an escape.

That is why this book is called *Setting your Sights*. Set your sights on the job you *really* want, the one to which you can contribute the most and the one which will give you the greatest satisfaction. By aligning your particular strengths with the right job, you will find yourself going forward smoothly. You will be equipped to surmount the obstacles and deal with the stresses that surface from time to time in any job. And you will be ready in due course to make the next step to another job — perhaps even a complete change of career — which may build on unexplored aspects of your character and attributes.

Happiness at work is a great clue to happiness in other aspects of one's life. You will be well, for one thing. Your partner will find you an easier and pleasanter person to be with, for another. Friends and colleagues will respond positively to you and your dealings with strangers will be enhanced by an easy openness and friendliness. Why is this? What each of us needs most, is the fulfilment that comes from exploring our potential to its utmost. The nearer we can attain to realizing our special attributes, the more in harmony we will feel with the world around us and the more we will find enjoyment and fulfilment in our work.

CHAPTER THREE

Self-confidence

As we grow up we accumulate, through circumstance, family, education, and society, a great many negative ideas about what we can achieve. We find it hard to be our real authentic selves when others have certain expectations that they project on to us. Parents may want their offspring to succeed where they themselves have failed and may try to push their children towards the careers they would have liked. Lack of encouragement may thwart the ambitions of others, especially when it comes to following an artistic or creative career. If you wish to act, write or become an opera singer, a certain amount of solid self-confidence in your ability is a critical factor, all too easily undermined by well-meaning parents, friends and teachers who advocate more stable and secure livelihoods.

In all sorts of ways we may grow up with a deep sense of inadequacy which may cloud the whole of our adult lives. In fact the way we perceive ourselves is perhaps the single most important factor in dictating our success or failure in life. Lack of confidence hinders our effectiveness at a very deep level. Even those who appear confident and who seem to have their feet firmly on the road to success, may turn away from real success when it is almost within reach. This often comes about through accident or illness or some other apparently outward intervention so that the deep psychological blockage is not immediately recognized. But often the real reason is a subconscious but persuasive voice saying: "You can't do this, you can't be successful; this job is for someone else, not for you".

It is not unusual for people to feel they are not as good or as capable as those around them. They come to expect failure and, feeling that they will never be successful, do not make a strong enough attempt to succeed. They may tend towards servitude and their natural willingness may lead them to do more than their fair share of dull, routine work. Such people may neglect their true mission in life and never come to fulfil their potential. This is often true of creative and intelligent people who lack conviction of their gifts and are unduly sensitive to criticism and easily discouraged by setbacks.

The price paid is enormous. Poor health, pain and discomfort, anxiety, tension, headaches, backache, insomnia, nightmares, indigestion, constipation, colds, obesity, alcoholism, fear, cancers, heart attack — people now suspect that these are some of the many life-damaging results of a thwarted, and un-satisfactory way of life.

New psychological developments have at last focused on individual potential. The language and practice of various modern movements in psychology may differ widely, but they share a common premise. People have an ability to create their own lives and fulfil themselves once they have become aware of the subtle ways in which their early life has conditioned them towards limited achievement.

The frustration caused to the individual by this conditioning actually uses up an immense amount of energy. Once freed from negative thought patterns and the behaviour they inevitably cause, that energy is released to help create the happy, alert, fully functioning person we all crave to be.

How does this help with getting a job? It's quite simple. The more authentic a person you feel, the more confident you will be. Confidence is the single factor most likely to get you successfully through an interview. Confidence is what will enable you to do your job well. Confidence will enable you to respond to flexible patterns of working. But this will not be empty confidence; it will come about through your discovery of your real self and recognition of your real worth and accomplishments without the deep sense of inadequacy that has been inculcated in you throughout your growing years. With this self-esteem you will find it easier to consider more flexible patterns of working and career paths, because who you really are will not be defined or circumscribed by your job.

Setting your Sights on Self-confidence

Use purposeful relaxation

Non-productive thought patterns begin to weaken their hold as you relax. Sustained relaxation will enable you to perform better at work and you will find yourself better able to cope with stress. Set aside time twice a day to relax properly and use this time to do some serious positive thinking.

Overcome mechanical thinking patterns

Try to become aware of any notion that is holding you back. It might be:

- – I'm no good at figures
- – I can't remember
- – I get so muddled when I'm under pressure
- – I can't concentrate

Examine these thinking habits. Many of them have little or no basis in fact. Like a computer, the mind can be programmed to think in a certain way. Most of us think negatively much of the time — a process which has probably started early in life. Old habits of thought, like all old habits, are strong and vigorous. The last thing they will do is lie down and die quietly. You will find, as soon as you decide to change them, that they are full of guile and subtlety, and you must make regular positive affirmations to change a lifetime's negative thinking patterns.

Awareness is the first step. Once you have become conscious of the thought patterns that are robbing you of confidence, make a note of them and start programming your mind in a more positive way. First, go into a state of deep relaxation and then begin by contradicting negative habits of thought. Use the present tense to make your thoughts more dynamic.

NOT
- I will try to get better at figures

BUT
- I am good at figures
- I can remember
- I cope very well under pressure
- I can concentrate tremendously well and make good use of all my time.

Think positively

Take a positive approach to your job search and look upon interviews as opportunities to meet someone new and to talk about something of mutual interest — the job you hope to be offered. Remember that the interview is a conversation with a purpose and this offers you a chance to find out about the job and the organization you hope to work for in the future.

The job search may be a long and difficult time for you. Keep positive thoughts in mind and if an interview goes badly for whatever reason, or if you think you won't get the job, put it behind you. It is not worth dwelling on all the things you should have said, but didn't. Learn what lessons you can from it and then leave it. Don't let it prey upon your mind.

Be single-minded

Whatever you are doing, do it fully with complete commitment to that particular activity. Often, we do nothing well because we are only giving it part of our attention while worrying about something else. Have you ever found yourself reading a book or a newspaper, and then discovered, when you put it down, that you have not taken in anything because of some other nagging worry at the back of your mind? Many daily routine tasks are completed in this way. But, whatever the activity, you will find it far more quickly and easily accomplished if you give it your full attention. It will be easier to remember things that have happened. You will also find that you have more energy available to you because your energy has not been dissipated in needless worry about something else.

Overhaul your values

What are your values? Where do they come from? Are they your own or do they come from your family or friends? Are you really expressing yourself and your own values, your own thoughts and opinions? Or do you take on the ideas of others out of habit, insecurity, or a reluctance to find your own way? Set your own standards; affirm your own values. Use every opportunity to say what you really think and discover how good it feels to be right behind your words. Your values will become a real source of energy and strength to you.

Avoid the companionship of misery

Who are your friends? Who do you spend your time with? It's worth thinking for a moment about whether your existing friends are giving you the support you need, especially at a time when you are making changes in your life. Are they negative, or cynical, or discouraging? Do they laugh at your ambitions? If so, you should limit your exposure to their negativity, cynicism, or discouragement. Prolonged periods in their company will undermine you and attack the self-confidence you are trying to build up. Don't spend your time with people who are depressed, out of work or stuck in a rut. Find people who enjoy life, people who have rewarding jobs, interesting hobbies. Find out about them, about their jobs, how they came to be doing them, what they get out of them. These are the people to cultivate, for a positive frame of mind easily communicates itself to others. These are the people who will be most useful to you. Really valuable friends are not jealous, gossipy, carping or disparaging. Really valuable friends will want you to succeed, will encourage you, feed your enthusiasm, stimulate your ideas and help you in any way they can.

Dare to be different

Perhaps your living or working habits are also outworn and stale. Do you do things in a certain way because your family did them that way? Do your habits, attitudes and opinions owe more to your upbringing than the sort of person you have now become? Revitalize your life by trying out new things, new ways of doing things, and by taking up new challenges. When you feel different from people you are with, try to emphasize that difference rather than diminish it. Being bold about the things that make you stand out from the crowd is one of the ways of finding a new confidence in yourself.

Be accepting of yourself and others

A firm belief in your own success will free you for ever from petty resentments or envy. There is no need to be critical of others — it's a waste of time and emotional energy. Say to yourself:

> — I like people and get on well with them. Everyone is unique and my experience is enriched by each encounter. I give credit and praise where it is due, and encourage others to fulfil themselves just as I am finding growth and fulfilment in my own life.

Reach out to others

Most of us go about wrapped up in our own thoughts and worries, paying little attention to others, but just a few moments of courtesy to others can pay dividends in boosting one's own self-esteem. Take every opportunity to talk to people to improve your outgoingness and interpersonal skills. Next time you go to the bank, buy a paper, or wait in a bus queue, take the opportunity to say a few friendly words to the bank clerk, newspaper vendor or fellow passengers. See if you can make your remarks pleasant, positive and upbeat. It's all too British to complain about the weather or to go on about how late the buses are; you will find you get a much more welcoming response if your opening gambit sets a positive tone. Once you have tried this approach a few times, see if you can keep the conversation going for a few minutes by showing an interest in the other person or by broaching a topic that has been in the news. Find out what others think about issues by listening carefully to what they have to say. Reaching out to others in this way can have a marked improvement on the value you put on yourself, *and* you may find that quite quickly you have enlarged your circle of friends and acquaintances.

If you feel you have little to say for yourself, read widely: newspapers, magazines, and books. Practise thinking about issues of the day and forming your own opinions about them.

Learn how to say "No"

Respect your own individual rights, needs and wants and be prepared to guard them by means of a little healthy self-assertiveness when necessary. Many of us feel bad about saying no, especially women who often feel they should be nice and kind and self-giving to others. Your parents, your spouse, your children, your friends and colleagues will all make demands of you and there will be times when you need to say no. Often the fear of saying no comes from a fear that there will be an angry and hostile reaction, but usually this is not the case. Most people are sympathetic to the needs of others and do not become angry when their requests are refused. To say no, make it clear that refusal of a request is not a rejection of the person making that request and say no on the basis of shared knowledge of your situation.

Say:

- No. I'd like to help you but as you know I'm too busy.

- No. I'd like to lend you my new sweater but as you know I'm rather jealous of it.

- No. I'd like to give you a lift but as you know it is out of my way.

Or, at the office:

- No. I'd like to help you [finish these letters/stay for the meeting] but as you know I have to leave by five-thirty.

Learn a new skill

One of the best ways of all to boost your self-confidence is to take up and succeed at a new challenge. Decide to brush up your French, understand figures, master the wordprocessor and become computer literate. These things will undoubtedly help you in the job market, but any new skill mastered is a bonus: how about learning to play a musical instrument or taking up a new sport? If there has always been an unrealized ambition to lose weight, take up painting, or write a novel, astound all your sceptical friends and find a new source of self-esteem by setting your sights on success.

Set your sights

Establish your goals and work hard for them. There can be no sustained change or personal growth without first clearly defining your goals. Write down all the things you want to achieve and change. Being as specific as you can, describe the qualities you need in order to reach your goals. Use your periods of relaxation to make positive statements about your goals and the personal qualities you need to develop to attain them. Take one goal at a time and work out a programme for yourself to achieve it. Only tackle other goals when you have

31

made some progress with the first one — otherwise you will be left with a number of uncompleted projects and you will have gained nothing.

Make a commitment to excellence

Make a personal commitment to excellence in all that you do and let excellence be your hallmark. Never turn in slipshod work. Take a pride in everything you do. Build a strong sense of self-respect by making sure every task is accomplished as well as you are capable of doing it. High self-esteem never settles for mediocrity. Begin with a commitment to excellence in your job search and believe in your own success.

CHAPTER FOUR

Preparing a Curriculum Vitae

There is no doubt that self-confidence in your own ability to do the job is going to communicate itself to the interviewer and enhance his confidence in you. This self-confidence must be real — based on knowledge of your own gifts and achievements and self-mastery of your drawbacks and limitations. Be honest. Bluff and boastfulness will quickly be seen for what they are by even the most incompetent interviewer.

Confidence comes through a lively and realistic appreciation of your qualities and skills. Make a list of your own particular attributes and and if you lay them out under the following headings, you will have the basis for your *curriculum vitae* or career history.

Identity and circumstances

Education

Training and professional qualifications

Employment record

Personal interests and social activities

This list serves as a useful framework, but it will pay dividends to flesh it out with as much detail as possible. In an interview, questions will be posed that will probe your career summary for details of your true personality and inclinations. This is where you must be rigorously honest with yourself because your personality is the most interesting thing about you and it goes on developing and being tested long after you've stopped taking formal examinations. There may be some aspects of your personality that you feel have not necessarily been highlighted in your past jobs and which you would like to exploit in future. For example, you may feel that you are good with people. If you have been in a very desk-bound job without much interface with clients or customers, this aspect of your personality may not have been noted very much.

Be frank with yourself about past mistakes and failures — what has experience taught you? If you can honestly tell an interviewer that you know you have had a poor record in the past for being over-impatient or have had difficulty in delegating tasks etc., and that you have now recognized the fault and been at pains to take positive steps to counteract it, you will be in a stronger position than someone who is reluctant to admit to any faults. Mistakes are only made by people who *try* things; there is some truth in the adage that people who have never made a mistake have obviously never made anything at all. A catalogue of self-justification or excuse is of no value to anyone. Deal with your limitations honestly, face up to them and counteract them it you can. Be strict and friendly with yourself. It's no good castigating yourself for being tone-deaf, but if you know you are lazy, well. . . begin at once to change that by taking full responsibility for yourself and what you can achieve.

Career change

Self-knowledge and accurate self-assessment will help you to concentrate on your strong points and give a good account of yourself in an interview. It may be instructive in other ways: perhaps your job is one that is not best suited to you — or to the person you have become.

One afternoon, when I was bored at work, I made a list of my personal qualities, and another of the attributes required for the job I was doing. The disparity was so great that it led, by various stages, to a complete career change.

It's not unusual to find that people who were rather shy and lacking in confidence at the beginning of their working lives have blossomed into sunny, strong-minded people by their late twenties or early thirties. A task-oriented sort of job that might have suited a young person still finding his feet may not provide the pace and challenge for a more mature person. Perhaps a more gregarious and people-oriented career would be worth seeking out.

By the same token, ambition comes to some people early and to others later in life. It is hard, but not impossible, to make a career change. Provided you have the determination and self-knowledge, you will succeed. But if your desire for change is just a whim to try something different, you may not have luck on your side. Restlessness is something employers are wary of and your motivation is likely to be probed quite deeply at an interview. Ask yourself why you want to change. What difference will it make to the way you see yourself? What difference will it make to the way others see you? Will there be a price to pay for what you want? Who will pay that price?

Self-Assessment

In order to be successful at interview, you will need to know just who you are and what you can do. If you don't think your philosophy degree is enough to get you a job, or feel down-hearted because you have been out of work for a long time, don't despair. You will need to think carefully about the skills and abilities you have acquired in your social or student life and you will soon find there are all kinds of experience that will be valuable to an employer — you just need to know what they are and how to present them.

Consider for a moment what activities are desirable in a work situation. **Planning** might be one of them. In a job you may have to plan your own time and that of others; you may have to plan a project or a new marketing campaign. If it is to go ahead then someone will have to draw up a **budget** for it. Then there is **organizing**, **setting priorities**, and implementing a critical path towards the finished product. To do this successfully you will have to **delegate** some of the work to others who will need **training** to do the job properly. Perhaps you will need to set up a team who will need to be **motivated** to carry out certain tasks in order to meet your deadline. The team will need **directing** and you will need to **monitor** their performance, **controlling** them if your standards or your budget are not met. It may be that you will have **negotiate** with someone about the hours that are worked on a certain project and if this causes conflict, you will have to **mediate** between the two parties concerned.

Now think about when you have had to do these things even though you it may not have been within the framework of a job situation. Make a list of these managerial tasks (adding others to your list as you think of them) and then set your own experience along side it. If you are a university or college leaver with experience of running a student society, for example, your lists may look something like this:

Planning Planning the term's activities, booking a hall or a room for your meetings, inviting guest speakers.

Budgeting Working out how much money will be spent on events, how much on printing leaflets etc.

Organizing Organizing your time, setting priorities, between running the society and keeping up to date with your work.

Delegating You may have to delegate to other members to publicize society events.

Training You may need to train (or get someone else to train) others to use special equipment, a film projector for instance.

Motivating Some special event you're putting on may call for extra effort clearing up afterwards and you will have to motivate others to help.

Directing You will have to assign different tasks to others in order to get all the work done.

Monitoring Perhaps you will need to monitor attendance records to see which events have support of members.

Controlling If the society is taking up too much time you will have to take control so your work doesn't suffer.

Negotiating   This is a skill you will have learnt if you have had to get leaflet printing or advertising cheaply, or if you have had to negotiate a fixed sum with a hotelier for the annual society dinner.

Mediating   You will have learnt this skill as chairman of any student committee. It calls for a certain flair for compromise and bringing about a win-win situation for both parties.

Chairing   You may have to chair a committee meeting to discuss the direction and aims of the society, its finances, or the simple day to day arrangements for running it.

If you are a housewife and mother, have you ever organized an event to make money for the local church or school? Have you tried to organize shared transport for getting children to school? Or a rota of child-minding or a baby-sitting voucher system? I am sure you have your own examples of things you have successfully organized for your community. Make a note of what they are. Now think about the skills you have employed to make this happen:

Initiative   You will have had to ask around amongst your friends or village residents

Assess need   to find out what is required and who would be interested in helping.

Assess resources   You will have had to discover what facilities they have available and what skills they can offer.

Plan   With your team you will have had to work out the best way to proceed.

Assess problems   Develop a contingency plan. Cope with last-minute crises.

Decision making   You had to decide who would do the work and get everyone

37

Leadership	working together as a team.
Budgeting	You will have had to work out costs,
Schedule	implement a programme,
Monitor costs	keep track of expenses,
Negotiate	try to get reductions.
Diplomacy	Perhaps people have let you down through personal reasons.
Listening	You will have had to discuss their problems sympathetically.
Evaluation	Others may have let their performance fall below an acceptable level (e.g. lateness).
Confronting	You will have had to talk to them and ask them to improve their effort.

Once you have made your self-assessment, keep it by you and keep it up to date. When you have secured your next job move, it will be helpful in preparing for appraisal interviews. And it will be a useful document to turn to again in a few years' time when you may be seeking either another move or a promotion. For now, your self-assessment will be the basis of your letter of application and c.v.

Self-evaluation exercises

Exercise 1: Achievements

Start to boost your morale by listing your achievements. Whether you are a school or college leaver, a housewife and mother planning a return to work, or a seasoned manager, your achievements are going to be your building bricks for your future career.

What counts as an achievement?

Count as an achievement, something you enjoyed doing, did well, and felt proud of. That is all. There is no need at this stage to consider how other people would rate them. To other people they may not appear to be particularly significant, but to you they matter because they represent something on your scale of values or because you have achieved something against a background of difficult or adverse circumstances. Review what you have accomplished in recent times and then work back to your earliest experiences. I hope you you can think of achievements from all facets of your life, whether it's your business, home, school, community or social life. Make it a good long list including all the things that you have done that you take pleasure and pride in looking back on.

This exercise should not be hurried. Give it time and thought. The thoroughness with which you marshal your material will ultimately pay dividends in heightened effectiveness in the interview situation.

Now, from your list select between five and ten of those you consider to be the most important to you. Remember that this is a subjective exercise and its value lies only in those achievements that are important to you. What the rest of the world may think of them need not concern you at this moment.

Take a separate sheet of paper for each of these accomplishments and set out in detail:

- what you actually did

- what you achieved (in terms of people, profits, savings, improvements, services, rewards)

- what you achieved in terms of the importance and significance of the achievement to your life: What did you learn? How did you benefit?

The final part of this exercise is to look through these pages and then list your achievements

a) in order of their importance to you personally.
b) in order of their likely importance to an employer

Exercise 2: Employment history

In order to decide the next step in your career, it will be helpful if you review your previous employment. Again, take a separate sheet for each of your previous appointments and list:

- the name of the company and type of business; the title/s of your position/s; dates of promotion/increased responsibilities; reporting relationships and your span of control.

- list what you think of as being your most significant contributions to:

  a) the job — it is not unusual for people to raise the status of their jobs by taking on extra responsibilities which then become part of the revised job specification. Have you done this in any jobs you have held?

  b) the company — have you implemented a new system, organized a keep fit club, set up an archive, found elegant solutions to problems that were being overlooked because they were not anyone's particular responsibility?

You may wish to include:

- specific problems or issues you have tackled and resolved

- general changes you have implemented or improvements you have introduced

- changes in style, organization, communication

- indicate the things you particularly liked about the job, and what gave you the greatest satisfaction.

- indicate the things you particularly disliked about the job, list any chores, or things you put off regularly or always preferred to delegate whenever possible.

- what did you do? List your duties, tasks and actual responsibilities. Quantify this information wherever possible — the number of subordinates, size of facility, budget, volume, sales/marketing targets, capital employed. Put down anything that indicates size, scale, or importance.

- do you have any specialized knowledge or skills? Book-keeping, law, pensions, computers, technology, for example. Were you frequently called upon to provide this sort of service or support for your colleagues?

- look back over your appointments and select the two or three that were most satisfactory to you. Try to evaluate why they were important for you, what sort of satisfaction did you derive from them. Don't overlook the social aspect; many people enjoy their time at work more because of their colleagues than because of the actual tasks they are called upon to perform. It may be that you function well within a small tightly-knit group of people and should look for a job which will give you this kind of community feeling at work.

Exercise 3: Personal biography

Self-knowledge will help you keep cool under fire. You will need to be well prepared to come through in-depth, or stress interviews. For this reason, you will gain an important insight into your personality if you understand the many factors that have contributed to your success and influenced your development.

- What are your true abilities, what really motivates you?

This exercise covers the whole of your life, from your earliest recollections right up to the present time. Give special thought to the relationships that have affected your life and development. How have the things you have done related to other people. Make a note of your approximate age at each experience. Use this exercise as an opportunity to elaborate on material you have put down in the previous two exercises, if you wish.

- Write a detailed biographical sketch of your life, beginning with your early childhood and including your school days and any further formal education. The sketch should take you right up to your first permanent job.

- Write a detailed account of your activities outside working hours. What have you managed to find time for in your leisure hours from your first job to the present?

- Review in detail your early experiences, including family life, school, and sports. Include assistance you have given to family, friends and others in your local community. What have you done for your church, or for social and political organizations? Were you a Scout or Guide, or a school cadet? Have you done any military service? What were your first money-making activities, how do you manage your personal finances now?

- Analyse and describe insights into relationships you established, the conditions surrounding your interpersonal and intergroup activities. How do you see others and what are your attitudes towards people? How do others see you?

- Write some notes on your personal philosophy. What are your values? What is important to you? What objectives do you set for yourself and how do you go about achieving them? What have you contributed to your own life, and what have you accomplished?

Exercise 4: Preferences

This is something of a fantasy exercise, but it has a serious purpose. You should take any or all of your past jobs and examine them for their good points. Forget, for the time being, about all the dull aspects of your previous jobs and concentrate on what you enjoyed. The chances are high that these things are what you are good at and should try to find in your next position.

- Write down all the duties, functions and responsibilities that you enjoy. This is not a job specification and it doesn't have to correspond to any particular job known to you. You should simply list the activities you prefer.

Exercise 5: Career progress

This exercise is an opportunity for you to examine your career critically. What would an objective outsider make of your career choices? Have you made wise, considered choices, or have you moved around in a number of jobs in your early twenties and now find yourself in your mid-thirties or older without a clear career path?

– Write down an assessment of your career to date. Evaluate the highlights, ennumerate your successes, but also take a critical view of the weak points. How could you have avoided these? Where does your career path need strengthening, what new experience do you need to gain?

Exercise 6: Adverse factors

Here is a chance to think about what may have held you back from achieving all you should. Perhaps there were personal considerations which frustrated your attempts to get on; perhaps events at work beyond your control limited your progress at a particular vital stage.

– Write down events or conditions in your personal life which may have hindered your progress at a particular time.

– Write down any events or conditions in your working life that may have hindered your progress. Such factors might range from an unsympathetic boss who would not delegate to a difficult home situation that prevented you from getting ahead. It may be that the company was the victim of a take-over resulting in the closure of your department at the very moment when your career appeared to be entering a growth phase.

– Write down any personal characteristics, habits, and traits you have that may be against you. Is there any aspect of your character that puts you in an unfavourable light?

- Write down any tendency you have which may draw forth criticism from your colleagues or superiors. Poor time-keeping, gossiping, or inadequate communications might be possible detractors from your career advancement.

Exercise 7: Interests and spare time activities

This is an area that is often overlooked in job selection, and yet how you spend your free time can be very revealing of character. Are you a workaholic who takes work home? Do you simply exchange office work for housework and, not setting aside time to replenish yourself, suffer an undue amount of exhaustion and that hard-done-by feeling? Do you slump in front of the television with a drink until oblivion sets in? Are you an enthusiatic sports player or do you have a passion for music, bee-keeping or watercolours?

- Write down what you do in your time away from work. What are your hobbies? Describe the activities for which you are prepared to find the time and money. How long have you pursued these activities? Do you take your interests seriously and make time for them or do they get put aside due to family or domestic pressures?

- If you are a workaholic who frequently brings work home, write down why you do this. Is it because you use work to hide from a problem at home? Is it because you manage your working hours badly and therefore feel permanently behind with your work? Is it because you are genuinely understaffed at work? If so, is this a problem that could be solved by recruiting new staff, sharing the work load with colleagues, or delegating to a subordinate?

Exercise 8: Long term goals

Few succeed without a very clear idea of where they're going. The effective pursuit of your goals is only possible once you have them very clearly in view. Set your sights by considering how you want to target the future.

- Write down your desires and plans for the future.
- What are your personal/professional goals for the next year?
- What are your personal/professional goals for the next five years?
- What are your personal/professional goals for the next ten years?
- What are your personal/professional goals for life?
- Which is your single most important personal goal?
- Which is your single most important professional goal?
- Are your personal and professional goals at odds in any way? If they are incompatible, which will you postpone or forgo, and for how long?
- Write down anything that may be preventing you from achieving your goals, especially any character traits that may be hindering your progress towards your desired goals.

Exercise 9: Money matters

- Write down your present earnings (or, if you are not currently employed, your earnings in your last appointment).
- How important is money to you?
- If your present level of remuneration is less than the highest you have earned, examine the reasons for this.
- What are your present earnings objectives?
- What are your earnings objectives for the next five years?

Exercise 10: Education, training and qualifications

a) Formal education

- Write down any periods of further education, whether at university, polytechnic or college of further education. List the subjects you studied, and the degrees, awards, certificates or diplomas attained.

- Write down the schools you have attended with dates, examinations taken with dates, and other school activities, sports, societies, and levels of school responsibility, eg: house captain, head of form, prefect etc.

b) Additional training

- Write down all additional training, including correspondence courses, evening classes, company-sponsored courses and seminars.

c) Practical skills

- Write down other practical training. Can you drive, type, do shorthand, cook, use a computer, do book-keeping, write well or have good design skills? Do you have badges or certificates for life-saving or first aid?

d) Self-improvement

- Write down all the things you have studied informally on your own and in your own time, whether it's photography, learning a language, making lampshades or playing a guitar.

e) Reading

- Write down the newspapers and magazines you read on a regular basis.

- Write down any books or articles you have read in the last two years relating to your work. Have you read books on, for example, economics, technology, computers, management, finance, sales negotiation or PR?

- Write down any other areas of expertise. Under this heading you might consider any special knowledge of products or markets, machines, equipment, systems, or processes.
- Write down any special abilities and skills. Languages, artistic talent, musical knowledge, or manual skills, should be listed here.

Exercise 11: Memberships and networks

Because a very large number of jobs are never advertised, it's worth trying to capitalize on your professional memberships and friendships. If you let your contacts know that you are looking for work, you will soon find that you have mobilized a very effective job-searching network on your behalf and you may be very pleasantly surprised by the results.

- Write down all professional, business, community or social organizations to which you belong, or have belonged at some time. State the length of your membership. How active are/were you? What offices do you or did you hold?
- Make a list of all the people you know who work in your chosen field. How well do you know them? Do you have any interests in common besides work? What positions of responsibility or influence do they hold?

Exercise 12: Personal circumstances

- Write down your age, marital status and dependants. Do you own or rent your home, run a car? Is any of your income derived from unearned sources?
- Write down an assessment of your own health. What is your height/weight, state of overall fitness? Do you exercise regularly, eat sensibly, limit your alcohol?

The Curriculum Vitae or Career History

Your career history can tell people exactly what you want them to know. It doesn't have to be utterly comprehensive — in fact it's better for it not to be. What you put down on your c.v. should be a selection from your self-assessment of those aspects of your qualfication and experience that are most relevant to the job you want. Your c.v. should contain no negative information whatsoever. Keep it brief, upbeat and positive. Take trouble over it: it might be the most important document you ever write.

The interviewer going through your c.v. will be looking for what he can use. At the back of his mind there is his checklist of desirable qualities required by the job — he has a pretty good idea of what sort of education, qualifications and experience he is looking for and these are usually stipulated in the job advertisement.

A chronological record of employment history with no gaps will inspire confidence, especially if it shows a steady progress of successively more responsible positions. You may feel that this is rather a bald approach and wish to flesh out your c.v. with more details of your specific skills and achievements. This kind of combination c.v. is especially useful if there are gaps in your career history and it is not necessarily a smooth progression from one thing to another. Don't worry too much if this is the case; it is true of many people. The point is to put over all the aspects of your life that are relevant to the work, but with this proviso:

Everything you put down on your c.v. must be true and accurate.

If you lie, deceive or exaggerate, it is more than likely that this will be found out at the interview stage and your chances of employment with that company will be ruined. If you practise deception and are hired and your deception is found out later, you run the risk of a very embarrassing dismissal. No one likes to be made a fool of and that applies to companies just as much as to individuals. It is naive to think that employers won't bother to check the information you put down, so be honest.

The practised recruitment manager will also be familiar with and on the alert for tricks of embellishment. Mis-representation of job responsibilies is easily encouraged by use of the words "managed" and "implemented" or "directed". Don't be in a hurry to use such words unless you know exactly what you mean by them and can back up your claims with real experience.

It may seem rather hard, but there are recruitment managers who, faced with a huge pile of applications, will use some quite arbitary means of reducing it to a manageable heap. One way is to lay them all out on the floor and throw darts at them, but a more serious method is to throw out any c.v. longer than one A4 page. I do know managers who adhere to this rigorously, believing that if you can't organize your material to get it all on one side of A4 paper, you haven't got the organizing abilities they are looking for. In fact it is a good discipline to restrict your c.v. to this length: on average only 15 − 20 seconds will be spent on it before a decision is made about whether to call you for interview or to put it on the discard pile. It is not necessary to go into great detail about jobs you have held in the past, but if you really find it difficult to organize all the information you want to put down, ask a friend's advice about what to leave out. If all else fails, try a typewriter with a smaller typeface and experiment with different kinds of layout.

What you need not say

The purpose of the c.v. is to secure a job interview and to that end you should discriminate carefully about the sort of information you put down. There is no need to reveal your age, for example, especially if you think it may go against you. In fact, mature people are increasingly in demand since research shows that they stay in the same job for longer than their younger colleagues, and that they are generally more conscientious. Having brought up a family, women returners are often much more organized and can do more work in less time than younger employees.

It's not necessary to put down whether or not you are married or have children, or any other personal or domestic detail. Nor should you feel you have to give your nationality, your political persuasion or your religion — unless you want to, or unless this sort of information has been specifically requested. Occasionally an organization seeking to promote a particular religion or political viewpoint will ask for applicants to be in sympathy with their aims and will give preference to those who are.

DOs and DON'Ts for drawing up your c.v.:

1　DO be honest.

2　DO keep it brief, no more than one side of an A4 sheet. Put only the information that gives a positive impression of you.

3　DO write your c.v. using power words wherever possible. Say: I was in charge of, I developed, I created, I instigated, I managed, I controlled, I ran, I had responsibility for, I supervised.

4　DON'T feel obliged to include your age, marital status, race, religion or politics.

5　DO put the most important information in the upper third of the sheet. Usually it's a good idea to begin with your most recent work experience and work backwards to your education and schooling. If you are still in full-time education and your only work experience to date has been vacation work, then you should list your vacation jobs in chronological order after details of your school, college and university attendance.

6　DON'T give away what you currently earn. Keep your earnings a closely guarded secret for as long as you can.

7　DON'T list your referees. There is absolutely no need for any employer to seek to take up your references until you have been offered a job. Say referees will be supplied on request. Your referees will thank you for not bothering them unnecessarily.

8 DO keep your list of hobbies and spare-time interests short. A long list may make people feel you're not serious about any of them and will certainly give them the idea you have no time for work.

9 DO be sure to give dates for examinations, awards, publications, employment, etc. and be prepared to produce original certificates if requested to do so.

10 DO include any service in the armed forces, and give your rank or commission.

AND

DO keep a photocopy of your c.v. handy, so that you can refer to it again before an interview.

Name   : Peter <u>Anthony</u> **DREW**

Permanent address   : 96 Belsize Park Road
                          Belsize Park
                          LONDON   NW3 8LN

Telephone   : 071-974 9368

Temporary address   : Flat 4
                          49 Selly Park Road
                          BIRMINGHAM   B29 3JX

Telephone   : 021-456 8826

EDUCATION AND QUALIFICATIONS

1986-1990   : University of Birmingham
                        : French B.A. Hons. (Class 2:1)

1988-89   : University of Besancon
                          (Year abroad as part of French course)

1979-86   : Hampstead High School
                        : 4 A Levels: French (A), English (A),
                          History (B); 8 O Levels

WORK EXPERIENCE

Summer 1987   : Omlette 'n' Salad Bar Chef

I was responsible for ordering ingredients and cooking the
omlettes. I supervised two assistants who prepared salads
and washed up. I was also responsible for kitchen hygiene;
the kitchen was visible from the eating area and had to be
kept immaculate at all times.

Summer 1988   : Courier/Customer Liaison
                          Sable d'Or Camping, France

I was responsible for customer liaison and the smooth running
of the camp site. I supervised three staff who looked after
the hire of canoes and other equipment.

Summer 1989   : Guide, Moet et Chandon
                          Epernay, Champagne, France

I was responsible for showing visitors around and explaining
the champagne-making process in English and French.

INTERESTS AND SKILLS

Clean Driving Licence
Languages: French (fluent), Italian (learning)
Sports: Swimming, tennis, running
Interests: Reading, especially French literature; wine.
I have good communication skills and enjoy working with people.
My summer vacation jobs have all involved a high level of
customer liaison.

Name	: Cecilia **PIKE**
Address	: 123 London Road ANYTOWN AT3 4BW
Telephone	: (0123) 456789

CAREER SUMMARY

Experience gained in technical libraries included early responsibility for budgets, supervision of staff and provision of technical information. Recent career progress, after gaining formal qualifications as a mature student, includes company research and provision of commercial information to major management consultancy.

WORK EXPERIENCE

JORDAN & JORDAN 1985- Information Coordinator	I had total responsibility for research and provision of commercial information to professional consultancy staff. I supervised 5 researchers and introduced computerization.
PICKWICK CO LTD 1979-84 Assistant Information Officer	I was responsible for day to day running of information unit including the provision of technical information, supervision of three clerical staff and budgetary control.
GLAXO 1977-78 Dept Assistant	Experience of all aspects of running large technical and commercial information office
PIG LABORATORIES 1974-75 Librarian (R&D)	Running small technical library service, including purchase of stock and supervision of part-time clerical staff.
RARE BREEDS LTD 1972-74 Library Assistant	Training in general library tasks; early promotion to more responsible duties.

EDUCATION, TRAINING AND QUALIFICATIONS

1981-84	City University (part-time) MSc Information Science
1975-79	Birmingham Polytechnic BA Librarianship with Science
1970-72	Luton College of Technology 2 A Levels: English, Biology
1965-70	Luton High School 3 O Levels; 4 CSEs

Name   : Penny BROWN

Address   : 56 Little Hill Street
                      CLEVEDON
                      Somerset   BS29 5DX

Telephone   : (0273) 56567

CAREER SUMMARY

Qualified hairdresser with three years' experience of running
high street salon. Wide experience of hairdressing for both
men and women, including cutting and re-styling, perming,
bleaching, tinting, dyeing, highlighting and conditioning.
During seven years at home bringing up a family, I have kept
up with the latest hairdressing styles and have been able
to supplement our income by private hairdressing in people's
homes and in the Hill Top Nursing Home.

WORK EXPERIENCE

A CUT ABOVE   I had total responsibility for unisex
Manageress   salon, including recruitment, training
1980-83   and supervision of staff.
Senior stylist   Awarded Institute of Hairdressers Design
1981-82   Award for 1982.

SCISSORS   Wide experience of hairstyling for men
Stylist   and women. Introduced new cutting and
1979-81   styling technique.

EDUCATION, TRAINING AND QUALIFICATIONS

GET AHEAD   City and Guilds 760 Certificate in Ladies'
Apprentice   and Men's Hairdressing with Distinction.
1976-79

1970-76   Clevedon High School
                    4 O Levels: English, Maths, Geography,
                    and Domestic Science.

INTERESTS AND SKILLS

Clean Driving Licence
Aerobics and Jazz Dancing

After my second son was born (1985), I set up and ran the
Twinkle Toes Nursery Club in the Parish Hall three mornings
a week.

I am good at organizing and have management and financial
skills. I especially enjoy working with people.

Name	: Paresh **SINGH**
Address	: 92 Long Wall Street LONDON SW11 4PZ
Telephone	: 081-234 5678

CAREER SUMMARY

Certified accountant with comprehensive experience of all aspects of accountancy in public practice with emphasis on computer audits, financial advisory services and client liaison

WORK EXPERIENCE

PITT, LAING & PARTNERS 1987- Senior accountant 1985-87 Semi-senior	Responsible for portfolio of clients, reporting to senior partner. Extensive client consultation, audit planning and control, staff co-ordination, accounts preparation. Familiar with tax and Inland Revenue requirements.
BROWN & MITCHELL 1984-85 Trainee	Gained broad business knowledge dealing with clients ranging from major quoted corporates to self-employed individuals.

EDUCATION, TRAINING AND QUALIFICATIONS

1984	Association of Certified Accountants ACCA
1983-84	Kimble College Professional exams 1 & 2
1982-83	Wring College Accountancy, foundation year
1976-81	Bedford High School 2 A Levels: Physics, Maths 7 O Levels

ADDITIONAL INFORMATION

Languages: German (studying)
Sports: Squash, cricket
Interests: Film, Classical Guitar
Clean Driving Licence

CHAPTER FIVE

The Job Search

In order to conduct a successful job search you will need to consider where to look for the sort of job you want. Where do employers look for the sort of people they want to hire? First of all, if the organization is large enough, it may advertise internally through a notice board or in-house magazine. Advertisements will also appear in newspapers, both regional and national; Sunday papers; periodicals (e.g. *New Statesman*) and professional or trade papers. However, periodicals and trade papers may not be very useful if they only appear quarterly. If the organization wants a certain amount of pre-selection done for them it may seek to recruit from Jobcentres and government agencies; private employment agencies; recruitment consultants, search consultants or 'headhunters'; school and college careers offices; or ex-service agencies.

You should be aware, however, that less than 40 per cent of job vacancies are advertised. The majority of jobs are found through personal contacts. Networking through your friends will often throw all sorts of unexpected opportunities your way.

Advertisements

A good advertisement should attract your attention by means of a clear headline that addresses you and your needs quite specifically. It should convey a reasonably clear and concise idea of what the job will actually involve and, possibly, how it will lead to advancement. Provided that the person recruiting has done his preparation, the advertisement should state which skills, qualifications, and experience are:

a) essential
b) desirable
c) helpful

A salary range should be stated. Failure to do this or a statement saying "salary negotiable according to age and experience" is often taken to mean "we pay as little as we can get away with", but such an assumption may be unfair. The salary may be genuinely negotiable especially if the company is hoping to find an unusual high flyer and is prepared to offer substantial perks as well as a good salary to the right person.

The firm should supply its address and telephone number and state how you should apply. Some companies only give box numbers, but this may be offputting to the great majority of candidates, and you may ask yourself why a firm should be so secretive.

As you read through the advertisement ask yourself whether it looks professional, is well-presented and is straight-forward and easy to read. Does the copy read as though the company is taking its search for employees seriously by being clear about what is required, and what is involved, and how it will reward the successful candidate?

School or College Careers Offices

Full-time employment is so different from full-time education that it is only to be expected that students will have only the vaguest ideas about the kinds of work they will be able to do and enjoy doing. If the students have some experience of vacation work that has given them some insight into and liking for a particular industry — working on a farm, for example, or in the catering industry, this may be of great help to them in deciding what sort of career to pursue. Those less fortunate must rely a good deal on what others can tell them and should consult parents and relatives and parents' friends, careers officers, and careers publications to find out as much as information as possible. Large corporates with several vacancies will be pleased to send a representative to talk to students. In addition they may have a video which will be helpful in describing what they do.

If there is a large employer in your neighbourhood, the chances are high that the careers officer knows a good deal about it and the sorts of job vacancies that are likely to arise. Someone from the company will probably be pleased to show you and a group of friends around and to discuss the possibilities of employment with them. Find out as much as you can about the work so that you have a clear picture of what is involved. You should also try to find out what kind of career progression there is if:

a) you are trained on the job
b) you undertake an apprenticeship or training of some kind with the company
c) you gain more qualifications before joining
d) you join a competitor

University Recruitment

Graduates are in great demand and those who have followed a discipline with some numerical content are likely to be able to start work at an average salary of £11,000 and more. If your field is computer programming or systems analysis, your starting salary may be twice that. Graduates are in the lucky position of being actively courted by companies as shown by the increase in job fairs, typically held in the autumn, at which companies explain what they do and how they work. These job fairs are also open to those who have already started work but who feel the need of an early career change as well as those who have left college or university and taken a year off to travel abroad or try short-term jobs.

Unlike the Milk Round visits made by corporates seeking to recruit large numbers of graduates, the job fairs may not involve active recruitment. Their purpose is to interest students from all years in the careers available in industry so that when they come to seek employment they can make a more informed choice. Companies attending the Milk Round, however, will expect to conduct first level selection interviews and may expect to recruit between one and five graduates from each campus as a result. Job fairs and Milk Rounds give students the opportunity to assess how professional a company is and whether their aims and objectives are compatible with the student's own values. It is not unusual, for example, for pacifist graduates to find they have inadvertently applied to companies which, among other things, manufacture components for the armaments industry. In these days of high ecological awareness, you may feel particularly strongly about a company's record with regard to environmental pollution.

A good employer should not be seeking to pull the wool over your eyes; there are good and bad aspects of every job so don't be afraid to ask what the unpleasant factors are. Perhaps noise levels are very high, for example, or you will be required to work unsociable hours. If there are recently-recruited graduates available, ask them how well the company has matched their expectations and whether they can see themselves staying with the company for a while.

The *Prestel* viewdata facility is available in many campus careers offices. This offers up-to-date and reasonably detailed information on current vacancies with major corporates.

Jobcentres

In a Jobcentre you will find cards on display advertising vacancies, but these vacancies will be mainly for manual skills or for junior clerical staff. There is nothing to pay by either the applicant or the employer for this service. Usually someone at the Jobcentre will make an appointment for you to have an interview once you have identified jobs you think you would like.

Jobcentre staff can help you with advice about careers and jobs in your area. Perhaps most valuable of all, they will know about training opportunities. There are now a great number of training schemes available and some offer practical work experience as well.

If you have been out of work for six months or more, ask at the Jobcentre for information about your local Jobclub. In addition to a few friendly faces and a chance to talk about your job hunting needs, you will find advice about tracking down the vacancies that are never advertised. Access to stationery, newspapers, directories, telephones, photocopiers and type-writers will help to make your job search a great deal easier and there will be people willing to help you practise your interview technique too.

Private Employment Agencies

The most common of these are large national organizations with offices widely distributed throughout the country (Reed, Brook Street Bureau, Alfred Marks, for example) though there are many, many small independent agencies as well. They mainly specialize in clerical and secretarial staff, but some have added more specialist services for accountants, for example, or hotel staff, publishing personnel, or linguists. If a successful appointment is made the employer has to pay a fee based on a percentage of the first year's salary; the applicant has nothing to pay.

Some companies build up a good relationship with the personnel of their local branch and will tend to turn to them often to fill vacant posts, thus saving themselves the trouble of advertising. The thinking tends to be something along the lines of "we had good people from them in the past, so maybe they can come up with someone good now". In order to keep up a steady supply of good applicants, the agencies may advertise frequently. The agency staff will interview you and will usually check your skills by means of a few simple tests. Depending on the level and seniority of the jobs they are trying to fill, they may also wish to see certificates of any qualifications you claim to possess and may take up references before putting your name forward for vacancies.

One of the frustrations of agencies is that if you see a job advertised by them and they decide not to put you forward for it, it can be very difficult to find out who the potential employer is in order to go direct.

If an agency does not have an opening for you straightaway, there is a danger that you will become one of a heap of names in a card index box on someone's desk and you won't hear from them again. Once registered with an agency, you should keep in touch with them frequently. Immediately after any interview they arrange for you, send them a thank you note, even if you do not get the job. Take an interest in them, cultivate them as friends. Make sure they always know how to reach you and let them know if you are going away for any length of time. If you go on holdiay, send them a postcard; if they are ill send them a note, and don't forget to send a card at Christmas. If you eventually find work through another means, write and let them know and thank them for their efforts on your behalf even if in this case it was not successful. If they specialize in the sort of work you are after, try to keep in touch with the staff fairly regularly, even after you have found a job. That way they are more likely to think of you first when something unusually interesting turns up.

Recruitment Consultants

Sometimes called selection or appointment consultants, recruitment consultants operate in a similiar way to the private employment agencies above except that they will be seeking high calibre candidates for management posts. To this end they will advertise, interview and test applicants in order to put forward a shortlist of three or perhaps four excellent candidates to the organization that is retaining them. The recruitment consultant will be responsible for checking credentials and perhaps obtaining references before submitting a detailed report on shortlisted candidates for his client. If an appointment is made, the employer will pay a percentage of the first year's salary to the agency. The agency's expenses in advertising and travelling etc. will be charged as extras to the client. The applicant should not have to pay a fee.

Search Consultants

Head hunters, as search consultants are sometimes known, do not advertise. They are expected to know who is the best in the field by means of trade publications and professional journals and their own extensive networking. Companies will go to them for candidates for high profile posts, perhaps the chief executive of a company, for example, where there are likely to be only a handful of people with the right qualifications and experience. Head hunters tend to build up a certain expertise in a particular industry or profession and they will supplement their knowledge by means of active networking in that particular field. The head hunter will make discreet enquiries about the integrity, professional standing and reputation of the candidate before making a direct approach. As the candidate will probably already be employed in some similiar high level post and is unlikely to be looking for a move, the whole process will be conducted with a great deal of subtlety and discretion. It is then the head hunter's task to try to make the new position appear attractive and to "poach" the candidate away from his current employer. The search fees will be a high percentage of the first year's salary, which, given the level of typical appointments, is a pretty substantial amount. To be head hunted represents a certain kudos and indicates that one is in the upper echelons of one's chosen career or profession.

The Grapevine and the importance of Networking

Never neglect the value of networking. Let all your friends and acquaintants know that you are looking for a new job and ask them to let you know if they hear of anything. In this way, you may be able to find out about a job before it is advertised and, if you are suitable, this will be of mutual benefit to yourself and the employer who will be saved the time and cost of advertising and interviewing several candidates. Remember that more than 60 per cent of jobs are not advertised at all, so firms expect to find a certain proportion of personnel through the grapevine and may in fact prefer this method of recruitment. It is cost effective for them as it saves them the price of an advertisement. Moreover, as soon as you approach them they know three pieces of vital information about you:

- that you want an interesting job
- that you are interested in them
- that you think well enough of yourself to write and introduce yourself to them.

To network actively, make a list of all your friends who are in work and what they do. Ring them and make a date for lunch or an evening drink. When you meet up, find out all you can about the company and what it does, what its markets are, what its objectives are and what it is like to work there. Before you say goodbye to your friend don't forget to find out who you should contact about a job with that company — and ask him whether he would mind you making reference to him when you follow up the contacts he has given you. It will be more effective if you can write saying something like this:

Dear Mr Hawkins

Philip Fraser gave me your name and suggested I contact you about possible job openings with the MNO Company Ltd.

If your friend is well thought of within the organization, it will make your application all the more worthy of consideration. Research has found that employers are drawn to people who share similiar values, similiar outlooks, similiar ideas about politics, ethics, dress, humour and standards.

When you get home write a sincere and friendly letter to you friend thanking him for his time and help. Ask him to keep you in mind if he hears of any interesting jobs coming up. Then, draft a letter to the contacts he has given you. Show the letter to your friend or read it to him over the telephone and ask for his comments. When you have arrived at a final polished version of the letter, make sure it is flawlessly typed and send it off with your c.v.

Don't forget to keep in touch with your friend and let him know how your job search is going. And always write a friendly little thank you note for any tips or help he gives you.

The Search

If you are in earnest about finding a job, you must make your job search as thorough and as regular as you possibly can. Your success in finding a good job depends very largely on how you go about it. An intermittent, haphazard trawl through the papers rarely pays off. Setting your sights requires strategy, discipline, persistence and preparation. You must be prepared to expend time and money to be successful.

It will help you if you treat each day as a working day: your "job" is to find a job and it can be a full-time occupation.

Here is a plan for a concerted job search:

7.00 am   Rise, wash, and do relaxation and positive thinking exercises to boost your self-confidence.

8.00 am   Breakfast. Dress smartly for your job search.

9.00 am   Go to public library; research careers; local companies, check out trade magazines and all daily newspapers for jobs in your field.

11.00 am   Introduce yourself to local job agencies.

1.00 pm   Have lunch with a friend who is working: pick their brains about jobs and networking opportunities.

2.30 pm   Check at public library, Colleges of Further Education, Universities and Polytechnics etc for short courses and additional training.

4.30 pm   Back home, have tea and prepare c.v.; draft speculative letters.

7.30 pm   Have a drink with a friend who is working; pick their brains about jobs and networking opportunities.

Bedtime   Set aside time for relaxation and positive thinking exercises.

Start as you mean to go on. Get up early and get going on the newspapers. The national dailies have certain days for certain types of job – creative and media, business and accountancy, education etc. Get to know which papers are good for the kind of jobs you want and on the day it comes out, go through the advertisements pages exhaustively, reading each one carefully and trying to evaluate what is required, and whether there are hidden snags to ask about straight away.

Job hunting through advertisements depends upon luck rather more than one would wish. The number of jobs available in your chosen field when you start looking for work is utterly in the hands of chance, though generally more jobs are advertised in the autumn and winter months than in the summer. Also unknown is the number of applicants. You may apply and get to the top of the heap straight away, but there may be several good calibre candidates when you apply and you may not be amongst the shortlisted candidates. Improve your chances of success by applying for as many suitable jobs as possible. It's a fiercely competitive market, so don't let any opportunity elude you.

Once you have identified a job advertisement you are interested in, go into action immediately either by telephoning to find out more about the job, ringing for an application form or sitting down to write a carefully thought-out letter and enclosing your c.v.

Once a week, at least, go to the local library and read through the job advertisements in the national Sunday papers, the local papers, and, especially, any trade magazines relating to your particular area of expertise. If you can afford it, it's a good idea to have your newsagent order your trade paper for you, or take out a subscription. Not only will it keep you up to date on job vacancies, it will also enable you to be well-informed about new developments in the trade when you go for an interview.

Keep an open mind as you read and ask yourself certain questions:

- Does this job sound interesting?
- Is it work I know something about?
- Would my skills and experience be relevant?

- What extra skills would I need to acquire?
- What does it pay?
- Is the job in a locality I would like?
- What sort of prospects might the job offer?

Don't get carried away on a tide of enthusiasm. You must also ask yourself:

- What are the drawbacks?
- Will I have to work odd hours?
- Will I have to travel a long way to work?

Job titles vary so much from one company to another that really going by job titles alone will not tell you a great deal about the job. Lists of qualifications and experience often seem daunting.

You may wonder whether there is anyone who will meet all their requirements. Some of these advertisements appear to have been put together by a group of people who gather together and ask themselves what qualities an ideal candidate would have. At the end of such a brain-storming session an advertisement is drafted and the committee sits back and waits for a paragon to respond. In fact some managers do believe that the ideal job advertisement should produce only one candidate — the right one. But experience proves otherwise.

If only those with the ideal qualifications applied, the field would probably be very small. One of the rules of applying for jobs is: never rule yourself out. Let others decide whether you have what they want. How suitable you are will depend on your merits relative to those of the others who apply. If no one has all the attributes listed as desirable, you may well be in with a chance. Even if a person is a complete match for the requirements, there may be some other reason why they're not hired — personality could be one reason, an interview that goes badly for them another.

If you can honestly say yes to the questions you must ask yourself as you read through the advertisement, then apply.

- Is it a job you know how to do?
- Would you enjoy doing it?
- Have you ever done anything similiar?
- Do your skills and experience match all of the essential requirements and at least 80% of all the other stipulated requirements?
- Are you able and willing to make up the shortfall? That is, if fluent French is required, are you prepared to bring yours up to scratch if it's not quite fluent at the moment?
- Is it a job you want?
- Does it fit in with your long-term goals? If so, motivation and enthusiasm will take you a long way towards it.

Don't be put off by too high a salary! This may seem to be strange advice, but it is especially necessary for women. All too frequently women shrink from applying for jobs they can do well because they feel the salary offered is too high — they're afraid the job is too high-powered for them. A high salary seems always to attract men, but gives women sufficient pause for self-mistrust — can I really earn that much? Remember that salaries depend on all sorts of salary scales operating within a firm. There is no virtue in being paid peanuts, and there is no sin attached to being rewarded handsomely for your efforts. If it's a job you can do, go for it. If you don't, others will and they may be less well matched for the job than you.

When you see something of interest, copy out the details carefully or, better still, photocopy it. Details like names, addresses and phone numbers must be exact when you make your application and the more often you copy them down, the more likely it is that a mistake will occur. A photocopy is better for another reason, too.

In writing your letter of application, you should use the job title you're applying for just as the advertiser has used it, and it will help if you mirror their language in describing your experience in the light of their job description.

Responding to a job advertisement

When responding to a job advertisement, do what it asks. Don't write if the advertisement says telephone — you'll be left behind in the rush; don't telephone if it says you should write. If it suggests you write or phone for an application form, do just that; there is no need to go into details about yourself and your background until you have the form. The purpose of the form is to elicit information about candidates in a way that can be easily compared and evaluated. Sometimes, companies may request that you send them a handwritten letter with a typed c.v. If it's your handwriting they want to see, then a typed letter won't cut any ice; in fact it may automatically disqualify you. Send a handwritten letter. Make sure it is neatly written on good quality writing paper. And don't forget to enclose the c.v. Most recruiters will disqualify those who don't get it all together.

Telephoning

When a company is in a hurry to recruit, it can save valuable time by asking for a telephone response to advertisements. It may also be the most appropriate way to select a shortlist of candidates for certain jobs, such as a receptionist, or any job where a good telephone manner really matters.

Whoever takes the call will have been briefed to ask everybody the same questions and to check off the replies on a form for ease of comparison. Having noted down who you are, where you live and how you can be contacted, the telephone interviewer will probably wish to know what you are currently doing, what attracts you to the advertised job, and how your experience and qualifications match up to the job on offer. There will probably be a space on the form for the interviewer to also note whether you sound interested, aggressive or apathetic, and whether you can express yourself in a clear and articulate manner without fumbling over details. This is where your practice will have made perfect, I hope, for though stumbling, hesitant answers may contain all the relevant information, an interviewer is more likely to plump for conviction and fluency every time.

Jumping the queue

It may sometimes be a short cut to make contact by 'phone, even if the advertisement says write. At best, you can introduce yourself to the decision-maker, get a name to write to personally and make a positive impression of yourself as someone with specialist knowledge and initiative. It may be worth doing if you are able to make a very pertinent and sophisticated approach, such as: "I understand that you are setting up a new office in Milan. I'm very interested in this as I have just finished a similar pilot scheme for [a rival company] in Rome" or, "I am interested to read that you are intending to launch a new magazine for account holders. I have recently been directly responsible for setting up a similar house publication with [a rival firm]."

But unless the advertisement is very specific and your inside knowledge very relevant, you may find you've taken a wrong tack from which it will be hard to recover. At worst, you could be made to look a fool, or a nuisance whose application will only be looked out for in order to dispose more quickly of it. So, if you're not asked to telephone, don't single yourself out in this way unless you are very very sure of your ground and confident that you can make a wonderfully positive impression.

CHAPTER SIX

The Letter

Letters of application are either written speculatively to a company you know something about and would like to work for, or submitted in response to an advertisement.

The speculative approach

Many jobs, sometimes, the best or most interesting jobs, are never advertised at all. It's always worth writing to a company where you would like to work. Companies will be flattered that you have taken the trouble to find out something about them and to write to them speculatively. Do not be discouraged if they do not have a vacancy when you first apply; something suitable may come up later and if you have already established an interest, then you will be high on their list when a vacancy does appear.

You probably know something about the company you want to write to already, but it makes sense to be as fully informed as you can so that you can target your letter as accurately as possible. Try to find a trade magazine that covers their business. That way you will have a clear understanding of their place in the market and the competition they face and this sort of knowledge will certainly prove useful in the long run. It is also worth looking up Extel in your local library, and sending off for a company annual report so that you know a great deal about the company.

Your chances of recruitment will be all the greater if the company is expanding or developing into a new area of business and your letter reaches them *before* a recruitment drive is implemented. But if you appear interesting or have relevant experience, you may well be interviewed anyway. No one wants to miss out on something special and seasoned employers know how hard it is to find good people when they are needed. Even if there are no immediate vacancies, a good letter should lead to an interview — and getting the interview is the hard part. With this book, you will know how to present yourself in a winning light once you're there.

Always find out who to write to and write a carefully targeted letter. A letter to a personnel manager who is not aware of any immediate vacancies arising is not likely to get you very far. Write to the director or manager in whose department you would like to work and address your letter to him or her personally. Ring up and ask the receptionist who to write to; make sure you can pronouce and spell the name correctly before you ring off.

Use good quality stationery for all your job applications. It shows that you have confidence in yourself. Draft the letter first and then set it out clearly on the page in neat handwriting or careful typing, always keeping in mind that presentation is as important as content. If you make a mistake, scrap it and start again. Your application must be perfect.

In your letter, explain succinctly who you are, what your educational and working background consists of and why you have an interest in that particular company. Don't have too fixed an idea of what you might do for them — the purpose of the speculative inquiry is to get yourself to an interview where you can discuss career prospects in general and your strengths in particular. It may be only after a meeting with you that a clear idea will arise in the manager's mind about how best to deploy you. Write something like this:

Dear Mr Hughes

I graduated from the University of Sussex in 1985 with a good degree in Modern Languages which I followed up with a teaching diploma. At present, I am teaching French and German at a private school near Bath, but I am now actively seeking a change of career. Over the past eighteen months, I have come to realize that I am more ambitious than I first thought, and I do not believe a teaching career will provide me with the interest, challenge, and financial rewards that I seek. Having given considerable thought to my personal skills and attributes, I feel that I could make a valuable contribution to marketing, management training, or personnel work.

I enjoy travel, and as I am anxious to keep up my languages (I speak fluent German, good French and have a working knowledge of Italian) perhaps marketing would provide the best use of my skills. I would be interested to meet you and to discuss career opportunities at XYZ plc with you.

I very much look forward to hearing from you.

Yours sincerely

Axel Morgan

Be prepared to be flexible and if you are offered a job with the company that doesn't quite fit in with your first ideas, don't turn it down without due consideration. Another offer may not be forthcoming and, besides, the job may have prospects for you that you had not previously considered. It may be a sideways step or not as temptingly rewarded as you had first hoped, but you may find it worthwhile to accept it anyway if the company is sufficiently dynamic. Once in a company, you can soon demonstrate your value and be able to work towards the salary and position you are seeking. Only knowledge of yourself and your circumstances will enable you to decide what's best for you. BUT do go into the matter carefully and find out as much as you can about the job on offer. It is not unknown for companies to welcome speculative inquirers with open arms and try to fob off on them a job they've been finding it hard to fill.

The Letter

This is the company's first glimpse of you. It should tell them a great deal about you, even before it's been read. Presentation really is important. Your letter may be one amongst several dozen — or even hundreds — of applications and a well-presented letter should stand out from the others in the pile. Use good quality white paper. Conqueror paper is readily available at most stationers and is worth the extra expense. The majority of employers are not impressed by coloured papers, but if you think it is a good way of making your application look different, make sure your *curriculum vitae* is on matching paper too. That way, you will make a statement about yourself and your application will be distinctive.

Always type your letter unless a hand-written letter is specifically requested. Use a clean typewriter and a good black ribbon. Never send a photocopy or duplicated letter, however many applications you are sending out. (A wordprocessor or good electronic typewriter with a memory can help here, enabling you to make specific changes to a standard letter and then printing the whole thing out again beautifully for you.) Make sure that it does not look wordprocessed though. The company must believe that theirs is the only job that interests you. There should be no spelling mistakes whatsoever, so if your spelling is wobbly, keep a dictionary by you. Look up all the words about which there could be any doubt. People often believe that they can spell (a very dubious proposition) and it's the very words they feel most sure of that are the ones which let them down.

Whenever possible, address the person by name. If the advertisement just says write to the Marketing Manager, ring the company and ask the receptionist the name. All you need say is, "I'd like to write to your Marketing Manager. Please would you tell me who I should write to?" Make sure you know exactly how to spell the name before you put the phone down. If the person you want to write to is a woman find out whether you should address her as Dr, Mrs, Miss or Ms, too. Many people don't mind but some people are very fussy about this.

Put your own address at the top right hand corner, then below it on the left hand side the name and address of the person to whom you are writing. It's polite to put their job title under their name too. Put the date across the page level with the bottom of their address. Like this:

25 Norton Road
BRIMSTONE
Glos GL10 8PQ

I. F. Stevens Esq
Marketing Manager
Bramwell and Boston Plc
High Street
SWINDON SN9 7HJ   10th October 1990

Your first paragraph should say where you have seen the advertisement and which job you are applying for. Like this:

Dear Mr Stevens

I wish to apply for the post of [use exact words from advertisement] as advertised in today's issue of [*The Guardian*].

Note

Always state which job you are applying for. The company may be recruiting for several different posts at once, so it will save any confusion if everyone concerned knows which job you're talking about, especially if you are applying to the personnel department.

It's polite to indicate where you saw the advertisement. The company may be advertising in more than one publication and it may be useful to the company to be able to monitor which advertisement had the greatest response.

Your second paragraph should give a brief outline of the salient points of your education or training, and your career to date. Say why your experience is relevant and why you are interested in the work.

If you have been out of work for a long time, tell the employer what skills you have acquired from your other activities, like this:

I enjoy working with people and my experience of organizing concerts as part of the fund raising initiative on behalf of the

St Helen's Hospice has given me the opportunity to develop good team building and people management skills. In addition I can offer a flair for oral and written communications, the ability to manage budgets and schedules, and practical experience of publicity and public relations.

Finish the letter by reminding them that your c.v. is enclosed, and saying you look forward to hearing from them. If you have begun your letter by addressing the person by name, you should close with "Yours sincerely"; only use "Yours faithfully" for "Dear Sir" or "Dear Madam" letters.

My c.v. is enclosed. I hope you will consider my application favourably and I look forward to hearing from you.

Yours sincerely

Lorna Tate

Application Forms

A number of job advertisements will ask you to write or telephone for an application form in the belief that this is the only way they can be sure of having all the information they require to be able to compare applications fairly. Just ask for the form, there is usually no need to give any details of yourself at this stage.

When you have the form, it is a good idea to take a couple of photocopies before you fill it in so that you can have a practice run. The form you finally send off should be neatly written and nicely laid out. First impressions really do count so make the form look as neat and as readable and as well presented as you can. Read the form and any accompanying instructions very carefully and try to fill it in exactly as asked. It is not unusual for companies to photocopy all the application forms it receives and to circulate them to a number of people. For this reason black ink is sometimes specified as it will photocopy more clearly. No matter how much you pride yourself on your eccentric and flamboyant approach to life, don't fill in the form in turquoise or purple ink if black is requested. Similarly, the questioner probably had a reason for wanting to know dates of all your O-levels or other seemingly inconsequential information. It is not unusual for application forms to seek information that a company would really only need to know if you were actually employed by them, your next of kin, for example. This can be trying but you will disqualify yourself if you put down anything that sounds flippant or sarcastic. Always answer as clearly and straightforwardly as you can.

Look at the spaces on the form. The size of the blanks you have to fill in is a good gauge of how much detailed information is required. Use this as a guide as to how much to write. If you find a whole half page is given for you to fill in a description of your present job, just one or two short sentences won't get you an interview. Put the information down in note form if you think that will be clearer; it will certainly enable you to get more facts in. You will have given a great deal of thought to presenting yourself favourably in your c.v. and you may feel that your career does not look so good set out on an application form. It is always a good idea to send your c.v. as well. Application forms usually state that additional information should be given on a separate sheet so write on the form: "Please see attached c.v." and staple the c.v. to the form so there's no danger of it going astray. Make sure you take a copy of the final application form before you send it off, so that you can refer to it before an interview. Also do send it off promptly; you'll get nowhere by sitting on it. If you have been given a date by which to apply, make sure you get it in well before then.

Sometimes these forms or questionnaires may be attempting to extract information for a more in-depth analysis of you than seems strictly necessary. For example, you might be asked to describe yourself as others see you, to give your height and weight (for health assessment), or to give your personal responses to hypothetical situations. It just might be the case that this type of form will give you more insight into the firm's corporate thinking than the form will tell them about your real abilities.

The interview invitation

You may receive a postcard or letter straight away acknowledging your application and promising to be in touch later on when all the applications have been assessed. But it is not unusual to receive no immediate response to your application. Then, if things are going your way, you may receive a letter inviting you to come for an interview. A date, place and time may be suggested, in which case, ring up and confirm that you will attend or, if necessary, make other arrangements that will be more convenient for you.

It may be that a letter will come asking you to telephone to arrange a convenient time for an interview. In response, work out dates and times that would suit you best before you ring up so that you can give an impression of being efficient and well organized. This phone call will probably be with the secretary of the person who will interview you.

Check, if you are in any doubt, whether there will be one or more people interviewing you and don't put the phone down until you can pronounce and spell their names correctly. Also get from the secretary their job titles or positions in the company. Be courteous and keep to the point in your call. Don't forget that first impressions count here too. It will only be to your advantage if the receptionist and secretaries have a favourable opinion of you at this early stage. They may well make a comment to the decision-maker, such as "She sounds efficient", which will stand you in good stead.

The telephone interview

The telephone interview is generally a preliminary conversation to help the interviewer to decide whether to include you in his/her shortlist of interview candidates. It is particularly useful to the prospective employer who is some distance from your home and who will not want to waste your time by making you travel a long way unless they are sure you are the sort of person they are looking for.

The interviewer may ring you at work, but you can be reasonably confident that they will be discreet and ask only closed questions — that is questions to which the answer need only be "yes" or "no". Such questions are not likely to be very revealing, however, so you may be asked to return the call at a time when you can arrange not to be overheard. If this is the case, either use a private telephone or a card phone — it is very embarrassing to use a pay phone and find yourself short of change — and make sure you have a piece of paper and a pen to hand.

The telephone interview will usually be a short call to check something in your application letter or c.v. that is unclear — perhaps deliberately on your part. You might be asked whether you are still working with the most recent employer listed on your c.v., for example. But there will be other questions, too. Your current salary may be one of them and you should very courteously decline to answer this by saying something like, "That is something I would prefer to discuss at a later stage". Most employers will find this acceptable and let the matter drop until an actual job offer is made.

What kind of questions can I expect in a telephone interview?

The first questions are likely to arise from your c.v. and will be for the purpose of checking dates of leaving companies and the reasons for leaving. If you answer these questions satisfactorily, the questions will follow on to try to establish your ability to do the job. It's quite likely that the interviewer has before him or her a check list of activities the job entails and, in order to see how closely you mesh with them, may ask what aspects of your work you find most enjoyable or which you regard as the most important. It is even more likely, however, that there is a criterion that must be fulfiled: relocation or travelling might be such criteria and so you would be likely to be asked something like: "There's a good deal of travelling involved in this job. Can you tell me how much travel you would consider too much for you?" or "I just wanted to make clear to you that the job is based in Aberystwyth. Will that be a major problem for you?".

Unfortunately, although it may seem every bit as stressful as a face-to-face interview, a telephone interview is not likely to result in a job offer. It is only an unexpected hurdle you have to surmount in order to get your name on to the shortlist of interview candidates. Your aim is to secure the chance of a meeting when your contribution to the life of the company can be properly assessed and your own prospects there explored. If these sorts of demands can be met, a good telephone interview should lead to a face-to-face interview.

Company morale

The letter or telephone call inviting you to an interview will be the first chance you will have had of assessing the company's interface with the public. Hopefully, your first impressions will have been favourable, and you will have more opportunity to get the measure of the company when you turn up for your interview. What are the offices like? Does it look a lively and interesting place to work? What are the people like? Do the receptionist, the secretary, the decision-maker make a favourable impression? Do they sound calm and efficient or harried and rushed? Are they courteous or abrupt? Are you made to feel welcome, offered tea or coffee, given a chance to look round, or are you treated as though your visit were an annoyance?

First impressions about the company are important and should not be ignored. What they can tell you about the company you may be about to join is something that is very difficult to assess until too late: company morale. Company morale is a frequently ignored aspect of work, but one which significantly affects the way employees respond on the job. Poor morale may result in excessive absenteeism and high staff turnover which will make your job harder. Low morale can spread like a canker through the whole life of the company and will affect even the most ambitious and well motivated person in an adverse way. It may mean that the company is not doing particularly well at the moment or that communications within the company are not of the best. A company which can generate high morale is one where people enjoy their work and feel that their efforts are contributing to the success of the organization. They feel that their work counts and is appreciated. High levels of morale are not only found in successful companies. It can be found in companies that are struggling to keep afloat as well as in young, enthusiastic start-up companies. The point is that people are responding well to challenges and feeling that their efforts are worthwhile and appreciated by the management.

CHAPTER SEVEN

The Interview

What is an interview?

Interviews happen all the time. They are really purposeful conversations during which one party tries to find out something in particular about the other. We have been having them all our lives, perhaps without realizing it and certainly without calling them "interviews". A doctor trying to establish what is wrong with a patient is conducting an interview. A teacher who tries to find out why a bright pupil has started failing exams is also conducting an interview. Anyone who has ever taken on one side a friend who seems upset or worried and tried to find out what was wrong has been conducting an interview.

Interviews will form a major part of your working life so it is a good idea to get used to making them work for you. Soon after you have been recruited your boss will probably conduct some kind of informal interview to see how well you are settling in at work. More formally, there will be appraisal interviews, probably on an annual basis, which will be used to review your performance, set future objectives and establish whether you need extra help or training. Any promotion that comes your way, whether it is with the same firm or not, is likely to entail an interview. You may soon reach a point where you become the interviewer; as you move into areas of greater responsibility you will probably have to conduct selection and appraisal interviews yourself. Whether you are the interviewer or the interviewee, you will find that thorough preparation is the key to success.

Ideally, a selection interview is an attempt to find out, by means of sensible discussion, whether or not you are able and willing to do a particular job. Ability and willingness are not necessarily demonstrated by the facts of your c.v. and application. Previous work experience is only a factual record. It does not demonstrate that because you have done something before, you are good at it — though this is often assumed. It is necessary to interpret these facts in the light of skills, aptitudes, attitudes, motivation and so on to see if there is sufficient congruence with the job on offer. The interviewer will be trying to find what you are like; to uncover your personality, behaviour and attributes. He will try to work out how you think, reason and solve problems, how you weigh information, apply your knowledge and arrive at decisions. He will also be interested to see whether you can communicate logically and clearly, how you express yourself and how well you respond to talking about yourself. What motivates and demotivates you, and whether you are flexible and adaptable will also be of interest to him. All the time you are being interviewed the interviewer will be both consciously and unconciously evaluating you: your body language and what it says about your confidence and energy levels, your self-possession, and ability to relate to others.

Generally speaking, interviews are a straightforward business, conducted in a courteous and friendly manner, and, unless proved otherwise, it should be assumed that there is good will on both sides. One must assume also that the interview is being conducted in good faith: that is, that the organization has a job to be filled and a serious intention of filling it, and that you, the interviewee, are genuinely interested in a job with that company and would give serious consideration to a reasonable offer of employment.

In trying to evaluate you, the interviewer will have in mind a list of skills or attributes that are essential for the job, others that might be desirable, and those that are actually undesirable. Fluent French or a clean driving licence might be essential; a certain level of numeracy or a knowledge of the market might be desirable. Colour blindness might be undesirable in certain jobs, especially where colour matching or safety is required. Your personality and ability to get along with others will also be evaluated. A difficult or prickly personality that might be tolerated in a valuable technical specialist may be considered wholly undesirable in a job involving a high degree of contact with the public.

The interviewer will want to know how gregarious you are. Do you enjoy team sports and events, or do you feel uncomfortable in a crowd and only operate well on a one-to-one basis? A job that involves marketing and making presentations to customers may not be ideal for you unless you are pretty outgoing and enjoy meeting new people. On the other hand, if the sales job also entails driving many hundreds of miles each week, this can make it a lonely one. Working at a computer or being a designer may also involve long periods of working by oneself without speaking to anyone. This requires a certain level of discipline and self-sufficiency.

Ability and willingness are not all that easy to perceive. Most managers have had no training for the task of interviewing and many unwisely decide to trust their own hunches: the "I'll-know-him-when-I-see-him" kind of approach which is nearly always unreliable in direct proportion to the complacency of the practitioner. It is a bizarre fact that although the health of a company depends upon the quality of its staff, and recruitment is therefore a key activity to the success of the organization, it is often performed by people with no training whatsoever.

A staggering fifty per cent of new appointments end within six months, which indicates that either selection processes are not very reliable, or that organizations assume applicants' knowledge of the job is greater than it really is. It is also true that the candidate can be misled, but this is almost never deliberate. It simply is not worth the time and effort involved in recruitment to set out deliberately to attract candidates who are unlikely to stay. It is more often the result of the mismatch between the candidate's own expectations of a brilliant career and the reality of the actual daily (often tedious) tasks that have to be performed.

Although recruitment is expensive, the cost to a company of poor selection is far greater still. Rapid turnover of staff due to poor selection is itself an immense cost: besides the resources that have to be set aside for recruitment, there is the intangible cost of delay, disruption, and low morale caused by unfilled posts on the staff. But the real cost of a wrong decision higher up the management scale is immeasurable. If someone is hired who is incompetent, the decisions that that person is hired to make may themselves cost the organization thousands of pounds each year. On the other hand someone with flair may make, or save, the organization many thousands each year.

Alternative methods of selection

Besides interviews, other means of evaluation currently being used vary from examination of handwriting or astrological anaylsis to psychological or personality tests which aim to determine your aptitudes and preferences. One suspects that they are often used because of the inadequacies of interviewers. It is certainly true that there is bound to be an element of subjectivity in a face to face interview and tests are therefore designed to make the outcome more objective. How effective these are is the subject of much controversy, but Warburgs, Royal Mail, and Pineapple Dance Studios (to name but a few organizations who use this method) prefer not to make management appointments without analysing the applicants' handwriting first. It is perhaps rather alarming that recruitment selection decisions about a person's personality and capabilities are made by the scrutiny of so limited an expression of it.

Anita Roddick of The Body Shop uses a special questionnaire to assess people's suitability. The questions, which appear unrelated to the actual job, include questions like what are your favourite flowers, or your favourite heroines in fiction. Other firms — amounting to 16 per cent of UK employers — may use more or less sophisticated personality and psychological tests, sometimes called psychometric tests, in an attempt to establish whether, for example, applicants for sales jobs are really as outgoing, gregarious and extrovert as they try to present themselves at interview. These tests can be pretty accurate and any attempt to manipulate the answers will be shown up by inconsistent results. The weakness of personality and psychological testing is that often the tests are purchased off the shelf, and not specially-commissioned to find out the precise attributes needed for the job. The danger of alternative methods of selection is that they may give undue weight to the wrong information and so may not uncover the attributes necessary for a particular job, though it can be argued that this is also true of the selection interview.

Another tactic used by some companies is to present a personality test to the interview candidate as soon as he arrives and then produce a print-out of the results during the interview and invite the interviewee to comment. In such cases the test itself may be of no real importance whatsoever. It is used to see how the candidate reacts first of all to having a test sprung upon him in this way, and then to the apparent "results" as they are relayed to him during the interview. Perhaps the "results" will indicate that the person is lazy or too domineering, for example, and the interviewer will be watching to see how good a case the candidate makes in his own defence.

A test called the Kostik Test, named after its inventor, invites you to select from a pair of statements, the one which seems to you to be the most true or the most accurate description of the job. Working to a strict time deadline you will have to compare and select up to 100 such pairs of statements.

If the job requires a manual or a professional skill, you may be asked to demonstrate your proficiency, and, provided you're not overcome with nervousness, this should be a reliable method of establishing your level of competence. For some management posts, companies try the "in-basket" test in which prospective candidates are handed an in-basket containing some of the tasks – letters, memos, telephone calls – a manager might actually come across in a typical working week. The candidate is supposed to go through each item and indicate what action he would take: whether to handle the task himself, delegate it, ignore it etc. How he manages his time, prioritizes the tasks, and deals with the material is noted and marked.

Leadership tests may involve getting a group of people over an assault course. Salesmen's skills may be tested by asking a candidate to demonstrate how he would go about selling a certain item of everyday domestic use, or how he would persuade a shopowner to buy a counter-pack for a completely new and untried product. For marketing personnel there are marketing games which try to get the candidate or candidates (this is sometimes done in a group) to set about the launch of a new product range. Where oral communication and personality are of particular importance, the job candidate may be asked to give a brief oral presentation on a subject of his choosing.

However, do bear in mind that these techniques of selecting candidates are rarely used in isolation and the inevitable hurdle is the interview, still employed by 99 per cent of British companies in the belief that it is the most reliable method of finding good quality personnel.

What has the interviewer got to go on?

Ability to do the job is probably going to be evaluated on a mixture of past performance, as far as the interviewer can uncover it, and "promise" as perceived by the good manager who knows not only what the job demands, but what a really good candidate could make of it. This is in the realm of guesswork since each job comprises a mix of tasks which may be different from the mix of tasks found in the same job at a different company. Track record of success in a previous job is not a guarantee of success in another job even though the responsibilities may be broadly similiar.

Provided that the interviewer is genuinely seeking the sort of information that will enable him to evaluate all candidates fairly, he will be asking you questions which should offer you an opportunity to shine. Seize them. And tell him about your achievements anyway. Many people lose the initiative because the "right" question doesn't come up in the right way. You may come out of an interview kicking yourself for not mentioning something that, in retrospect, might have been decisive. However much you value modesty, unfortunately there is no guardian angel sitting by your side at an interview who will blow a trumpet for you. You cannot expect the interviewer to divine your achievements telepathically. He or she must be told all the information that will enable them to decide that you are the person they wish to appoint. And the only person who can be relied upon to tell them is. . . YOU. If, at the end of the interview, you feel that there is some important and relevant piece of experience the interviewer has overlooked, then say so. The interviewer will generally ask you for questions or whether there is anything that has not been covered and this is an opportunity to say something like: "I would like to tell you about the vacation job I took last summer because I think the experience was very relevant to the job you have on offer. It gave me useful experience in dealing with customers. . ." etc.

By the way, the interviewer will be concerned to try to evaluate you fairly along with all his other candidates, so you should not be surprised or dismayed if he takes notes while you are talking. It is the only way he can be sure that he has asked everyone the same sort of questions. You may also wish to produce paper and pencil to note down any factual information you are given about the company. It's a good idea to have prepared some of the questions you want to ask too; have a note of them handy so that you won't forget to cover all the points of interest to you.

Personality

In addition to ability and willingness to do the job, the interviewer will also have to consider your personality. He will be looking for self-confidence, alertness and vitality. People who seem dull or dozy will lose out here. Though initiative is probably high on the list of desirable qualities, for most jobs it will have to be tempered with the ability to get along with others in a co-operative team environment. You must be able to communicate clearly — good verbal and written skills are vital to the workplace, so it's important to practise them whenever you can.

Employers naturally look for people who will be a good fit with the people already working there. The interviewer will have special inside knowledge to help him make this decision. If the staff tend to be rather extrovert people, dressing in a relaxed way, and being very informal, he may hesitate to bring in someone who is shy and conforming. The job on offer may not actually require an extrovert temperament, but if that is the "culture" of the organization as a whole, the interviewer will be concerned that the newcomer may feel unhappy and not settle down. It may be that the person to whom you should report has a highly idiosyncratic temperament and special personality traits of tolerance and diplomacy are required for the ideal candidate in addition to the satisfaction of the basic job requirements.

Assuming that the interviewer knows what your qualifications are, your past achievements and aspirations, his questions relating to your personality will probably be trying to probe something much more abstract. To answer these you must have done your homework for all these questions really come under the heading: "What sort of person am I?" By thinking hard about your true personality, you will be better prepared to describe yourself fluently in an interview situation. Be as searching, even self-critical, as you can in your assessment. Ask close friends to help you by listing the things they like and dislike about you. (There should be an even number of likes and dislikes, say six of each.) Ask them to give you instances of your behaviour. For example if a friend says you are well organized, make sure you have an example of a time and circumstance when you have created that impression. You will find actual examples enormously useful in an interview so always be ready with evidence of your claims. If you say: "In a group, I'm happy to take the initiative", be prepared to back it up with instances of when you have done so.

What is a good interview?

Generally, you will know if you've had a good interview. You will feel that the interviewer was genuinely interested in your application, was well disposed towards you, and that you were given the opportunity to do yourself full justice. Your own self-esteem will be left intact. If you were not the successful candidate in the end, you should be left with the feeling that the person who was offered the job must have deserved it even more than you did. Believe, too, that whatever happens is for the best. If you did not succeed in getting that job, it can only be because there is something better coming your way and you must be patient until the time is ready.

Coping with nervousness at interviews

Everyone has a deep need to feel appreciated and valued and, consciously or unconsciously, we look for appreciation at every social encounter. We may feel nervous of going to a party just because we want to be liked and fear rejection. But interviews are particularly nerve-racking. There is the strain of meeting someone for the first time in a strange environment. Then there is the additional stress of knowing that you have just about an hour to make a sufficiently good impression for them to offer you a job. Fear of rejection is exacerbated by fears of appearing foolish or ignorant. We may feel that all the power is in the hands of the interviewer and this is a further source of tension. It is so easy to feel like a helpless victim of another person's judgements, or whims. Rejection in any social context is a threat to our self-esteem, but rejection at the end of an interview may also mean a continuing lack of financial security or promotion. We may therefore feel rejected both socially and professionally.

You will undoubtedly fare better at an interview if you can cope with your fear of rejection first. When someone is nervous, the whole body becomes tense, especially in the neck, throat and shoulder area. Movements will seem jerky, thought processes slower and less lucid, for nervousness makes the whole system seize up — just as a car engine does not run smoothly when it is cold. There is a tendency to close up in a defensive way with the arms across the body. Not only does this body language clearly indicate to the interviewer that you are ill at ease, but it will also have the effect of making him feel more tense and ill at ease, for nervous people breed nervousness in others.

To overcome this tension, think of yourself in an interview situation, sitting across from someone whom you do not know who is asking you many searching questions about yourself. Try to imagine how you will feel in this situation and then begin consciously to relax any muscles that have become tensed. Concentrate on your breathing to make sure that it is deep, even and slow. Then tell yourself:

- I am powerful and can influence my path in life. My success is assured.

Practise acting in a confident manner, holding yourself up straight and walking tall. If you practise looking confident you will be more confident, for the language of the body can influence the mind, just as our minds can influence the body. An actor learns to overcome stage fright and develops a knack of turning apprehension into an asset by using the energy of fear to become a vital, expressive being on stage. In much the same way you can learn to influence your mind so that you grow in confidence until your "stage debut" at an interview.

During your job search, try to keep interviews in proportion. There are all sorts of ways in which you can create a career for yourself, so try not to go to interviews with a "do or die" attitude. Above all, don't take rejection of your application as a rejection of you personally. Stay powerful by reiterating your own commitment to excellence and do the best you can. Maintain your energy and self-worth by keeping fit and active. Boost your morale by making sure you are clean and neat at all times, not just on the way to an interview. It can seem unnerving to be dressed up for an interview, expecially if you normally wear jeans and a T-shirt. It's a good idea to acclimatize yourself by making an effort to look reasonably smart at all times. It will increase your self-confidence if you can wear a smart suit for an interview without feeling ill at ease.

Ready, Steady, Go!

Be there at least five minutes' early if you can. Being unpunctual is a slight — and you should not be kept waiting too long without an explanation either. If you are still waiting after 15-20 minutes, you should politely ask the receptionist whether you will have to wait much longer. Don't be kept waiting an unreasonably long time without an apology or explanation. Do you want to work for a company that doesn't respect your time and is prepared to waste it? Be polite, but firm, and suggest that you would be willing to come back later if the time set for the interview has suddenly proved to be inconvenient after all. There may be a perfectly reasonable explanation for this; even the best run companies have crises from time to time.

Use your waiting time constructively. You will probably be sitting in an area where the company has given some thought to its image and PR — is it clean and smart? Are there brochures or annual reports or any other promotional materials for visitors to look at? Sometimes you will find trade magazines and from these you may be able to pick up a useful last minute bit of information on one of their competitors which you might get a chance to ask about later — "how will your marketing strategy change now that RST is bringing out a new line in widgets?"

Probably a secretary will come and fetch you. As she shows you into the interview room, step forward with a smile and introduce yourself by saying your name clearly as you shake hands. Introducing yourself helps the interviewer to see that you are a self-confident person with self-esteem. It also saves the interviewer from making the embarrassing mistake of inter-viewing you as though you were someone else — quite possible if the interviewer's desk is awash with applications.

After the introductions, you will be invited to sit down and perhaps offered tea or coffee. Sit down where indicated unless the chair is awkwardly placed. In this case, pick it up boldly and put it down in a more sensible position. Accept tea or coffee by all means if you would like a hot drink. If you are feeling very nervous indeed, don't bother; drinking it without slurping or spilling it will just give you one more thing to worry about. On no account accept an alcoholic drink. It's quite likely that you're not being offered alcohol in an outburst of friendly hospitality but in an attempt to sleuth out your drinking habits.

To put you at your ease, the interviewer may try to make some conversation about your journey, or about the weather or some major item of the day's news. Reply appropriately but don't allow the conversation to spin out too long. You're there to get a job offer, so don't give the impression that you're reluctant to come to the main point of the meeting.

Good manners at interviews

You expect courtesy and consideration from prospective employers; for example, you would expect them to let you know if they had to postpone your interview for any reason. In turn it is only reasonable that a prospective recruiter should receive the same courtesies from you. Always telephone if you are not able to keep to an arrangement and try to give as much notice as possible. If you decide you do not want the job you should always let the recruiter know if you wish to withdraw your application, again giving as much notice as you can, rather than leave your application hanging in mid-air.

Be truthful at all times. Deliberate falsification of your age, qualifications or experience or any other information is just cause for an employment contract to be terminated.

It should be understood by both parties that the information that is supplied by either the prospective employer or the candidate may be confidential and that confidence should be respected. Sometimes at an interview, a recruiter may reveal a piece of information which he feels you, as a candidate, should know, but which he does not wish to become known in the world at large. If he requests you to keep that information confidential, you should at all times respect the trust that has been placed in you.

Appearance and body language

What your body says about you may influence the outcome of the interview more than we care to think. At least 50 per cent of all communication is actually nonverbal, so how you look, stand, sit and conduct yourself is crucially important. In fact, research suggests that less than two minutes will elapse before someone meeting you for the first time will have formed an opinion of you. And, as everyone knows, first impressions are powerful and long-lasting. Think critically about how you dress, walk, smile, shake hands and speak. Practise these things in front of a mirror and ask your partner or friends to give you a few hints about how you can improve your body language. You will find that standing and sitting in a confident manner will actually give you more confidence and make you seem more alert.

Clothes

An interview is not a party or a fashion show, so don't overdo things. However to look professional you must be smart and well-groomed. Your clothes need not be expensive, but they must be immaculate. Work out what your interview outfit will be and keep it in good order, ready, if necessary, for an interview at short notice. There is no need to have more than one interview outfit if your budget is tight and don't be embarrassed about wearing the same outfit for a second interview. It is more important to look really well turned out than to try to impress people with the size of your wardrobe.

It is a good idea to dress conservatively. A man should wear either a suit, or jacket and well-pressed trousers. Learn to iron well: a crisp, well-pressed cotton shirt always looks neat and smart whether it cost £6 or £60. You will be taken more seriously if you wear a tie. Footwear can really let you down — you know the expression "down at heel". Make sure your shoes are clean and in good repair.

A woman should wear either a suit or a well-cut skirt (not too short) with matching jacket. Somehow jackets always create a more professional impression than a dress. If your hair is long, tie it back or even put it up to achieve a sophisticated look. Jewellery should be discreet; no one will be impressed by armfuls of clinking bracelets or earrings dangling down to your shoulders. Do wear make up; lots of heavy eye make up is not a good idea, but the discreet use of blusher and a good lipstick will make your face look more alive and interesting. Take a spare pair of tights in your handbag so that you can do a quick change if you ladder your tights on the way. Hands and nails must be clean and cared for. Don't wear bright nail polish unless you can guarantee pristine results. Chipped or badly applied nail polish will lose you a lot of points.

Making an entrance

As you enter the room, you should carry yourself well. Walk tall with your head up. Look open and friendly and give the interviewer a genuine smile, looking into his or her face as you do so. Say your name clearly and distinctly as you extend your arm for a handshake.

Shaking hands

You may not have given much thought to your handshake before; do so now. Ask your friends what they think of yours. Many people who have the most off-putting handshakes, are completely unaware of the fact. The worst style of handshake is the dead fish we all know and dread. It gives an impression of a weak and flabby personality, which may be quite undeserved.

If yours is the strong-armed, aggressive knuckle-grinding sort of handshake, try to get your friends to help you modify it to something more friendly. The aggressive handshake creates an impression of a dominating personality and is not likely to make your interviewer warm towards you.

A good handshake conveys self-assurance and tells others you are pleased to meet them. Take the other person's right hand in your own with a firm grip, but without squeezing or pumping. Smile confidently as you extend your hand and make eye contact. Shaking hands with someone while looking past them or at someone or something else is very off-hand and should always be avoided. Looking pleased to meet someone will automatically create reciprocal feelings in the other person so that they will feel warmly disposed towards you.

The interview panel

If you are being interviewed by a panel, you will have to face a situation even the most extrovert and confident dread. You will be shown into a room of people who will probably be trying hard not to look too friendly. If the panel is more than three people, it's quite likely that you are being interviewed by people who feel self-conscious about their own behaviour in front of their colleagues. They will be taking a critical view of all the candidates so don't worry unduly. This is a superb opportunity to demonstrate your own poise.

Have you ever been impressed by someone shuffling into a room looking apprehensive? No. So don't do it. However nervous you are, the trick is not to show it, but to present a lively, confident self to the world.

As you enter the room, pause for just a fraction of a second. Hold yourself erect, with your head up. Smile a genuinely warm, friendly, open smile as you quickly look round the room at each face in turn. Having non-verbally greeted each one, step forward to where you are invited to sit. Stand tall and walk confidently across the room. If there are more than two or three people, shaking hands may be rather strained. While you should not refuse any hand that is offered to you, it may be a good idea not to rush into handshakes all round. Acknowledge everyone present as you are introduced by looking directly at them with a confident smile.

Even though questions may be coming at you from all sides in a panel interview, treat everyone individually and direct your answer to the questioner, maintaining eye contact as you do so. Try to take your time so that you can give a thoughtful and considered answer to each question. Refuse to be hurried or fussed. There's no harm in pausing for thought before you answer a question. If, when you have answered a question, the whole panel gazes at you silently, keep your cool. This is an old ploy to get people to give themselves away. Just say something like: "I don't think I have any more to add just now" or "I think I have answered that question as fully as I can" and wait calmly for another question.

Stand up to be noticed

It will occasionally happen that you will be shown in to the interview room on your arrival and asked to wait until the interviewer comes to join you. Magazines and perhaps coffee will be provided while you are waiting. By the time the interviewer comes into the room, you will be sitting comfortably in a chair with your magazine — and it is very easy to go on sitting there. However, to create a powerful positive impression, get up as soon as the interviewer enters the room so that you can greet him or her standing up. If you are a man and the interviewer is a woman, you should do this anyway as a natural courtesy. If you are a woman and the interviewer is a man, this courtesy is not strictly necessary; women are not expected to stand up for men. However, we know that it takes only two minutes for someone to form an opinion of you. You will make a much more significant impression in those fleeting seconds if you put down your magazine, rise to your feet, and give a confident smile as you extend your right hand for a handshake. If you are a woman being interviewed by a woman, perhaps even a younger woman, it will still make more of an impact if you rise to your feet to greet her.

Are you sitting comfortably?

Take the chair offered to you and sit upright with your case, folder, or handbag on the floor by the side of your chair, or on a side table if there is space available. Don't put it on the interviewer's desk; it looks like an infringement of territory. You will look alert and interested if you sit up leaning very slightly forward towards your interlocutor/s. Folded arms will create a negative impression, so keep your hands on your lap and though you may want to emphasize a point with your hands, try not to gesticulate with them too much. You want the interviewer to concentrate on what you are saying and wriggling or waving your hands around can be very distracting.

Most companies will want to make you feel welcome and comfortable; the days when interviewers played games with chairs — his high and imposing, yours small and low — are mostly over. However it is possible that the chair offered does not suit you; perhaps it is placed awkwardly, is too near a radiator, or faces into a light that is too bright for comfort. Have no hesitation in saying so and moving the chair to where you will be more at ease.

Seeing eye to eye

Eye contact is one of the major ways you can make a serious and business-like impression. The expression "seeing eye to eye" holds an important truth in our instinctive judgement on people. It means: "I like you, I am interested in you, I am confident and relaxed, honest and sincere". Looking away from someone has the opposite effect and says: "I don't like you, I am bored by you, I am nervous and tense, deceitful and insincere". These pre-judgements may be quite incorrect and undeserved, but nevertheless it is worthwhile trying to counteract a bad impression.

While you are talking to someone, try to imagine a triangle on the other person's forehead. The base of the triangle will be formed by the person's pupils, and the apex will be in the middle of the forehead. This triangle is the area where you should focus your attention whenever the other person is speaking. This will give the other person confidence that you are taking a lively interest in what he is saying and listening carefully to his questions. Try to focus on this triangle whilst you are speaking, too. The idea that good eye contact is an indicator of honesty and interest is so pervasive that there is a danger that the more your

95

gaze wanders from the triangle the less serious will be the impression you create. If you only focus on the triangle for about a third of the time, for example, you run the risk of being thought either shifty and unreliable, or morbidly shy and nervous.

A prolonged steady stare can also be uncomfortable, but this hardly ever happens. Whether people are talking or listening, they tend to break eye contact instinctively when they want to think, imagine or remember something. A conversation will naturally be punctuated by periods of eye contact, and periods of looking away, as the other pauses to recall and reflect. Once you have become aware of the importance of eye contact, you will begin to observe how people interact in this way, looking at the person to whom they are speaking as much of the time as is comfortable, with breaks in eye contact signalling moments of contemplation.

Mannerisms

Everyone has some mannerisms or bad habits that have become completely ingrained. When you are nervous at an interview some of these mannerisms may come out without your realizing it and they can be distracting, if not downright off-putting. They can be eradicated, but first we have to recognize them. A video is one way of seeing our behaviour through others' eyes, but it is not always an available method and unless you have recourse to one regularly, it will not help you to progress. Instead, ask your friends to tell you what bad habits they have noticed and enlist their help in overcoming them. Discover from your friends which is your most maddening habit and ask them to make a signal to you everytime you do it. They should also keep count of the number of times you do it on any one occasion. For example, do you play with your hair? Ask your friends to snap their fingers every time they see you do it. It is very distracting and even uncomfortable to see people touching themselves — picking their nails, touching their faces, scratching their hair, or adjusting their clothes, twiddling their rings, playing with earrings or other pieces of jewellery. Try not to fidget, doodle, drum your fingers, or click pens. Have you ever been riveted by someone twirling rubber bands, tearing a bus ticket to bits, systematically destroying some inconsequential item, or smoothing out a sweet paper? Yes, it is distracting, isn't it? What about verbal mannerisms? Try to watch out for "I mean", "kind of" and "like, you know", "OK" or any other little habits of speech that you have. Your friends can help to single them out and bring them to your attention by signalling to you every time one slips out.

To smoke or not to smoke

If you are a smoker and slightly nervous, getting through an interview without a cigarette can be gruelling. It is best not to light up unless the interviewer actually offers you a cigarette. Even then you should refuse if no ashtray is readily to hand because how to dispose of the ash and later the cigarette butt will become a distracting and embarrassing problem for you.

If you really do smoke heavily, you should ask what policy there is about smoking in the office. Many offices are now "No smoking – clean air" zones by popular request. If you are serious about wanting a job there you may find you have to be serious about giving up too. Other non-smoking employees will be rigorous about making sure you don't smoke — especially in an open-plan office.

Interview strategies — Keeping the interviewer interested

A lively interview should take the form of a conversation with a purpose. The interviewer will want to direct that conversation by asking questions that will lead to the information he needs to have in order to assess you fairly along with the others on the shortlist. Listen carefully to his questions. Just as not reading the questions on an examination paper can lead to lost marks, so you can lose ground in an interview by not answering the questions properly. If you have not heard the question properly ask the interviewer to repeat it. If you have not fully understood the question, say so and ask for clarification. Try to see what the interviewer really wants to know, and give an expanded answer whenever appropriate.

For example, take a simple question like this:

- What are your responsibilities in your present job?

Possible answers might be:

- I work in the Personnel Department and I report to the Personnel Director.

- I work in the Personnel Department where I am responsible for training. I have to evaluate the training needs for the company, find suitable instructors if there are enough people to merit an in-house course, or seek out the most suitable courses that will meet individual needs. Naturally I have to prepare budgets for the approval of the Personnel Director, to whom I report directly, and the Managing Director who takes a great interest in training.

- Well, we have recently installed a complete desktop publishing system in order to cut down our typesetting and page make up costs. I've been responsible for making sure people know how to use it effectively so that it can be operational in as short a time as possible.

Of the three answers the first does no more than indicate one relationship in an organogram. As an answer it is factual but does not contain enough information to be useful as an answer to the question. The second answer sketches in the main job description of the present job holder and indicates a reporting chain. It is useful and informative. The last answer describes a specific task without making clear whether these are typical duties or a one-off assignment. It could be the description of a freelance task, especially as it does not indicate a reporting link or set the job in the context of the organization as a whole. The second answer is the most appropriate reply, but the third answer would be a good response if the interviewer were to follow up with: "Can you give me an example of a training programme you have implemented recently".

You can help the interviewer is his assessment of you if you can add more information that shows him what sort of person you are. To do this, tell him what is interesting, enjoyable, rewarding or challenging about what you do or have done. So another possible answer would be:

- I was lucky enough to join the Personnel Department at a time when the Managing Director had decided to make a big commitment to staff training. I have to evaluate the training needs for the company, find suitable instructors for our in-house courses, or seek out courses that will meet individual needs. Naturally I have to prepare budgets for the approval of the Personnel Director, to whom I report. I find it very interesting to work in a large organization where the training requirements are so varied and I particularly enjoy being given quite a lot of scope.

This answer rounds out the facts with information that reveals the interests, attitudes and motivations of the interviewee. An expanded answer like this creates a positive impression and helps the interviewer to get to know what you are really like.

Opening gambits

The interviewer may take some time over your c.v. before asking questions. A frequently-used opening gambit is:

- I wonder if you would quickly take me through your c.v., please.

It may seem rather pointless — even annoying — when your c.v. is in front of them, but you are in fact being handed a useful opportunity to flesh out the vital information hidden in your career history. This is your chance to tell your questioners what you want them to know. It's well worth giving it some thought in advance and practising your answer. That way you can offer a smooth assessment of your career with motivations and achievements subtly interwoven.

> – I joined ABC's management training programme straight from university, and after two years I was sent out to Oman as part of a small team to launch a new product. It was a good opportunity for me and I enjoyed a year there as part of a brand management team very much. I've learned a great deal from working at ABC, but I feel that it's time I moved on — Oman was a high point and there's nothing coming up in the near future that offers comparable experience. I'm now ready to take on more responsibility and having had some experience of computer systems I think computer selling offers the challenge I'm looking for.

Such an answer may be probed for further information. "What sort of responsibilities and challenges are you expecting from this job?" for example.

Interview questions

The purpose of the interview is to gather enough information to be quite confident of hiring you to do a specific job. Depending on the competence of the interviewer, the information actually gathered will vary widely from one job interview to another. The purpose of this book is to help you to succeed at interviews regardless of the proficiency or otherwise of the interviewer. An understanding of the interviewer's techniques will help you to realize what the questioner is really trying to find out and the hidden agenda that may be operating.

Closed questions

Many of the questions you will be asked are closed — that is the question will begin with the words: Do you, have you, are you, were you, did you, could you, would you, is it, was it. The answers are going to be either "yes" or "no" or very short limited answers such as:

Question: How long were you at Bloggs?

Answer: Three years in all.

Closed questions may be used to check the information you have offered on your c.v. or to cross check some new information you have given during the interview.

– You spent five years with DEF?

– You speak fluent German?

Closed questions will also help the interviewer to test your commitment, and if you want the job, the answer is usually going to have to be "yes". For example:

– Are you prepared to work late?

– Can you start before Christmas?

– There will be some travel involved in this job – do you mind spending time away from home?

Open questions

These are questions that cannot be answered with a simple "yes" or "no", but must involve a more lengthy and considered response. Most of the questions you will be asked will fall into this category, but they may be patterned with closed questions. For example,

– Can you make snap decisions? (closed question with the appropriate answer "yes") may be followed by:

– Tell me about a time when you had to make a snap decision? (an open question demanding a full response from you).

- Was your decision accepted?

- Was it the right decision, do you think? (both closed questions)

- How did you arrive at your decision? (open question, over to you).

Open questions always begin with: Why, how, what, or, tell me about. . . They will have a conversational ring to them: "Tell me about yourself, your college days, your spare-time interests." Provided you have prepared your case thoroughly, open questions will offer you the best chance to shine. The person asking open questions is saying in effect "I am interested in you, in what you think, in how you do things, and why. Please tell me more about yourself."

The interviewer is therefore giving you the freedom to tell your story in the way you want. In this way he will be able to find out quite a bit about you and the way you operate, your motivations, energy levels and expectations. As you speak he will evaluate both what you say and how you say it. Can you structure your answer, for example, and give it a logical shape; are you forthcoming about yourself, or do you give the impression you have something to hide; are you alert and articulate, or vague and confused; is your thinking clear and concise, or do you ramble and become enmeshed in details? What tone of voice or attitude to yourself do you adopt when you are talking about yourself: are you self-deprecating, ironic, caustic, thoughtful, provocative?

The more preparation you have done, the more effectively you will be able to answer. Although stumbling and slightly hesitant answers are often the most informative and revealing, an interviewer is more likely to be impressed by conviction and fluency. Valuable specialists and creative people sometimes have a weakness in this respect when it comes to getting their ideas across. This why it is useful to think out what you want to say and practise it to the point where it seems second nature to you.

Moral questions

These questions may be a round about way of testing your integrity and may be asked in a hypothetical way. For example, "Which is worse, do you think, to steal five pounds from a large successful company, or to steal five pounds from a poor old lady of meagre means?" The question is really a trick, tempting the interviewee into dangerous waters. The answer, of course, is that stealing is absolutely wrong, and not relative to the victim's financial standing.

A similiar technique may be employed to find out whether you're weak-willed, easily-led or an inveterate "yes-man". In this case the interviewer will make a statement that is either clearly wrong or only partly correct and ask for your agreement. The timing of it is part of the game, it's calculated to catch you off guard. Some examples are:

- I always think one should treat suppliers with the contempt they deserve, don't you?

- The customer is always wrong unless his bill is paid, don't you agree?

- I find marketing men hardly ever know what they're talking about, don't you?

Note that the question is phrased as a statement with a little closed question tagged on to it to provoke a "yes" answer. This type of question often gets a reflex "yes" answer, out of surprise, politeness to the interviewer, and a wish to avoid controversy in an interview situation.

You may feel that the question is rhetorical and not worth answering, but silence may be taken for agreement. Good humoured dissent is the best way to deal with them. Say, "no" clearly and follow it up with a positive statement. Say, for example:

- No, I don't agree. I have always enjoyed a good relationship with my suppliers.

- No, I can't agree with you. I think it's important to treat customers courteously at all times.

- No. The marketing men I've come across know their job pretty well, I think.

If you keep a pleasant tone in your voice, you will find you can dissent without causing offence and you will have won respect for voicing your views.

While we're on the subject of moral questions, don't ever let yourself be drawn into gossiping about people in an interview. You and the interviewer may find you know the same people — not at all unlikely if you're both in the same business — and the interviewer may make an opening gambit inviting you to criticize or disparage someone. It may follow along the lines of the questions given above, "I think Evans is a fool, don't you?" Whoever Evans is, don't go along with this; keep your own counsel. Never be tempted to bad mouth your ex-boss either. You will be respected for not gossiping and your loyalty will be appreciated.

Why do you want to leave your job or why did you leave your last job?

This is a commonly-asked question and it requires a careful answer. Keep your responses as brief as possible and strike a positive note. If you are still employed, make it clear that you are looking for a new job because you are interested in a new opportunity. Never sound desperate to leave the old job. Concentrate positively on why you want the new job:

- This job interests me because I am seeking more marketing experience.

OR:

- This job offers me the sales experience I'm looking for.

The personality clash

If the real reason for your leaving your last job was a personality clash with your boss, wild horses shouldn't drag this information out of you. The chances are that this sort of personality clash is going to arise at some point in everyone's life, but the information will be bound to alarm a prospective employer, and may ruin your chances altogether.

Redundancy

Only jobs become redundant, not people. But all the same it is hard not to feel at a disadvantage when the question of redundancy arises at an interview. There really isn't any point in trying to dodge the issue. Say frankly that a redundancy situation arose, or that the company went through a phase of contraction. If the interviewer is persistent, however, you may be asked why you think you were made redundant when others in similar positions were retained. Say something which deals with the redundancy question, focuses the interviewer's attention back on your expertise and willingness to do the job, and reminds him again why you want the job. For example:

- My job became redundant and though I was offered another job with the company, I was reluctant to make a sideways move. I have valuable skills and experience to offer [say what your strengths are] and I would like to use them at a proper level of responsibility. When I saw your advertisement for a product manager, I felt that my experience would be extremely relevant.

What if you've been out of work for ages?

The hardest part of being unemployed for a long while is trying to convince people that "unemployed" does not equal "unemployable". Everyone who has been unemployed for any length of time knows that looking for work is a full-time occupation — seeking out opportunities, writing letters, formulating c.v.s, researching companies and attending interviews is very time-consuming. Unfortunately, no employer is willing to acknowledge this fact and expects the unemployed person to be full of good works and self-improvement. If your interviewer asks what you have been doing since your last job, say that you have been devoting a large proportion of your time to looking for the right opportunity. Obviously, you don't want any old job, you want one that will help you get on.

- I feel that I have a lot to offer and I have been looking for an appointment where I can make a positve contribution. This vacancy is one that interests me very much because my skills and experience are particularly relevant to the post of . . . .

But what else have you been doing? If you can say that you have kept your hand in by doing some freelance or part-time work, so much the better. Perhaps you've been on a training course, learnt a language, taken up bell-ringing or some other interest. Have you helped a group of volunteers restore a long-forgotten canal, helped to run a community project or redecorated the village hall? Travelling abroad is acceptable too, especially if you have been somewhere unusual and done some exploring by yourself. A package holiday in Lanzarote is not worth mentioning, but a two-month tour of Africa by bus and train probably is.

It's important to try to present yourself as someone who is energetic, organized and interested in the world beyond the hearth. The longer you have been out of work, the more important it is to be able to give a dynamic impression of someone who is time-conscious and purposeful. If you haven't done so already, take up some new activity without delay. The chances are that no one will ask you when you began it and you will impress prospective employers with your initiative.

Stress interviewing

A barrage of quick fire, tough or trick questions is designed to keep the candidate off balance. This style of interviewing handled by someone proficient at it, will help them to evaluate how poised you are, whether you are quick-witted and can think on your feet. For some jobs, these attributes are obviously necessary and the style of questioning may be appropriate.

If the candidate is exposed to this sort of treatment, the interviewer should take care to seal off the experience, so that the candidate does not find him or herself back on the street with jangling nerves and feeling very distressed. That is, he will bring the conversation back to a more friendly and co-operative level. If the job is one where you can expect a high level of stress and criticism, these methods will be something you may have to get used to. Salesmen who may have to field criticisms of a company's products or service may be particularly exposed to this kind of interview. It is not necessarily a reliable guide: the same person who may vigorously defend the company to clients may crumple when personally attacked.

If your job is one where there is no undue pressure, or exceptionally high stress levels, there is no real need for stress interviewing to be employed. There are still some interviewers who firmly believe that you can only really assess what a person is like by making them squirm, attacking their values and opinions and making out their achievements are trivial. You can always walk out. That won't get you the job, of course, but if you are being interviewed by a bully who is enjoying your discomfort rather too much for a job without high levels of stress, you may well decide you wouldn't want to work for that person anyway. It may be more useful for you to salvage your self-esteem. Incidentally, is not at all unusual to find that this kind of stress interviewing back-fires and the candidate, having come through with flying colours, declines the job offer, having been thoroughly put off by the interviewer.

Stress interviewing will test your quick wits and quick thinking. They will probably consist of several rapid questions and may appear to have nothing to do with the job. They often reveal more about the interviwer than anything else.

The stress questioner may be fairly young — mid-thirties — and sharp. He (this type of questioner tends more often to be a man than a woman) may have risen quite quickly in the organization and have gained a considerable amount of re-sponsibility early. But, despite this, he remains rather immature and may even have some deep-seated feeling of inadequacy. The method of getting on was probably established in his school days and consists of scoring points and trying to show up the opposition in a poor light whenever possible. Now that they have some authority, they try to emphasize their power by treating the interview like an interrogation. Their manner may be a disconcerting mixture of friendliness alternating with coldness or even hostility.

This kind of interviewer may have given some thought to how to present candidates in a disadvantageous way. If this is the case, tell-tale signs are a chair lower than theirs, a light that shines on you while their own face is in shadow. The candidate's tension may be increased quite sharply by seating the person in such a way that there is an open space — a door or window — immediately behind them. If you suspect that the room has been arranged to make you feel small and uncomfortable, an awareness of the fact will help you to counteract it. Sit very upright to minimize the effect of the low chair and actually move the chair so that the light does not disturb you.

The stress interviewer is a bully, of course, and if he is to be your immediate boss in the new job, you may be given considerable pause at the thought. On the other hand this type is generally weak and will crumple in confrontation.

The technique of the stress interviewer will be blunt and sharp:

- What makes you think you can do this job?

This question tries to imply that you're not quite up to it; speak up firmly about your abilities, your experience, and your enthusiasm for the job.

- Are your exam results a true reflection of your abilities, do you think?

If your results weren't so good, stress that you have other things to offer, mention your experience and your interest in the job. Don't fall into the trap of trying to justify poor exam results, you might find it only leads to further bullying. Remember that many successful people have not distinguished themselves academically at school or university.

- Where do you see yourself in five years' time?

"In your job", may not go down to well. Say something like this:

- I should like to be associated with a successful company, responding positively to change and developments in the market-place.

To a more mature candidate the interviewer may say:

- You're rather old to be applying for this job, aren't you?

Don't be fazed by this, after all you are being interviewed for the job so they haven't ruled you out on grounds of age. Relate your own particular skills and experience to those required by the job and stress your interest in the job.

- Why have you stayed so long with your employer?

This question is implying a lack of initiative. Make it clear that while you were being trained, making progress in your career and being given increased responsibility you had no reason to think of moving.

- Let's see, (counting through your c.v.) you've had three jobs in the last five years. Why have you moved around so much?

This question is implying that you are restless. Make it clear that each move represents a planned career move and that you have gained wide experience and advancement by moving on quickly and this experience is relevant to the job on offer.

The stress interviewer has some idea at the back of his mind that he is getting behind your guard, peeling away the mask, revealing the real you in spite of all your defence mechanisms. There is another technique he will use to discomfort you.

The ploy of silence

Silence is part of the stock in trade of the stress interviewer, but it's not only used by the bully so it's very useful to know how to deal with it. The silence ploy begins with the interviewer asking you a question requiring only a short answer. You answer. Silence. You say something else. Silence. You're very tense by now and say something else. Too much. You've blown it; you've now given him something else to bully you about. He asks you another stress question. Like this:

Q   Why aren't you earning more?

A   I'm on a fixed salary scale.

Silence.

My salary is subject to six-month reviews and, if I stay on, I would expect to be on a higher grade after January.

Silence.

Of course, money isn't everything.

Q   I see. You're not interested in money then. So we needn't pay you much. What is the minimum you'd be prepared to work for?

From this position it will be hard to negotiate your new salary, if you were to be offered the job.

The only way to cope with the silence ploy is to demonstrate your poise and remain calm and composed. The silence technique is not unlike the childish game of seeing who can outstare the other. If you remember it's a kind of game, you'll find it easier to cope with. In your mind, cut the interviewer down to a manageable size. Pretend you are looking at the interviewer from the wrong end of the telescope so that he appears very tiny, or imagine him as a baby wearing a nappy and playing with a soft toy, or sitting in a huge chair so that he appears small and insignificant. Keep calm and look expectantly at the interviewer putting pressure on him to break the silence. So a successful re-run of the above sequence would go like this:

Q   Why aren't you earning more?

A   I am actively seeking a position where my skills, abilities and experience will be rewarded at a proper level of remuneration.

Silence.

Q   What do you mean by a proper level of remuneration?

A   I would prefer to discuss that at a later stage.

Rules for dealing with the silence technique:

1   Recognize what's going on.

2   Stay calm.

3   Cut the bully down to size in your imagination.

4   Keep your answers upbeat and positive.

5   Never offer excuses or justifcation.

6   Maintain silence.

7   Glance expectantly at the interviewer, but don't attempt to outstare him.

8   Look bored if the silence goes on too long.

9   Keep the pressure on the interviewer to break the silence.

10 Remember that this ridiculous situation is of his making. Remind him that you have answered the question and say: "I don't think I've got anything else to add at the moment".

CHAPTER EIGHT

Interview Questions

Job title and salary

It will be of interest to most interviewers to know the date of your joining your last company (and the date of leaving, if you have already left), your job title, and your starting and present salaries. The reason for asking for salaries is so that the interviewer can see whether your previous employer has rewarded your performance levels with above average increments. The assumption is that a jump in salary is indicative of your worth to that company.

It will be greatly to your advantage when it comes to negotiating your salary package, if you can keep your actual salary to yourself. You may say that last year your salary rose by ten per cent, but do try to avoid mentioning specific sums of money.

The date of leaving one job and starting another can present a problem if your employment has not been continuous. Your c.v. may indicate that you left one job in 1987 and took another that same year. But if you left one job in January and did not take up another until December, the prospective employer will be quick to realize that you have had almost exactly a whole year less experience than he first thought. Be prepared to justify this gap with some activity that demonstrates your initiative or shows the employer that you have kept up your skills and kept abreast of developments.

What kind of experience do you have?

Having established how many years' experience you have, the interviewer may ask what *kind* of experience you have. This is quite a tricky question and one to which you will be glad to have given some prior thought. The amount of experience you have does not really tell anyone much about your work because many jobs only call for the same experience to be repeated over time.

The questioner is seeking a qualitative answer and trying to establish whether there has been progress in your career or whether you have had ten years of repeating the same experience that you gained in the first two years.

This is your opportunity to bring in past experience that may not be totally job-related. If you have been out of work for some time or if you have not had a permanent job before, the quality of your experience in organizing a family or running a society is not to be overlooked.

A woman who has been out of work for a number of years bringing up a family, for example, may be put off by thinking her non-working years don't count from an employer's point of view. If you treat those years as though they don't count, the employer will too. Show that your time bringing up a family has had value for you in job-related terms and that they have given you confidence in your organizational skills, time and energy management, budgeting awareness, and interpersonal expertise.

Your answer might go something like this:

- I left school with A levels in English, Biology, and Music and followed my parents' example in taking up a medical career. I went to the Westminster Hospital and became a SRN. Later on, I regretted this; I did not enjoy nursing and I think I was too much influenced by my parents — my father is a radiographer, my mother was a nurse — in taking up a nursing career. I married early in my twenties, and began a family soon afterwards. While the children were small, I went to a local college of further education and learnt lamp-shade making and found that this was a way of making a little extra money for the family.

- I sold lampshades on a regular basis to a small shop in the town and became a close friend of the proprietor and sometimes helped out in the shop, and I often did special window displays for her. When she fell ill and had to have

113

several months off work, I helped to run the shop until she was well enough to take it over again. This gave me experience of shop management. I was responsible for ordering and stock control and I built up a good relationship with suppliers and customers — in fact turnover went up slightly during the six months I was solely in charge, compared to the same six months in the previous year.

Go on to remind the interviewer why you are applying for the job by saying:

- I am interested in managing the Design Interiors shop because I have extremely relevant experience. I am familiar with the merchandise available on the market and I have a good understanding of customers' needs as well as good working relationships with the major suppliers.

A statement like this gives the interviewer the clear impression that you are someone who knows the value of your skills, and where you are going and the best way to achieve your aims. It also sounds dispassionate and gently reminds him that there may be some competition for your employment.

Broadly similar functions may be called by different job titles in different organizations. If there is any doubt about terminology you may find yourself being asked questions like:

- What are the responsibilities of a [eg.] project manager/editor/project co-ordinator?

- What are the most desirable qualities in a good [eg.] secretary/sales assistant/marketing manager?

These questions should be handled with care. The interviewer will have given a great deal of thought to the qualities he or she is looking for and will have compiled a job description. Even so, there is no one right answer and the interviewer will be impressed if you can show that you have thought hard about what you do.

- Likes and dislikes — what bores you?

- What do you dislike most about your present job?

- How do you cope with those aspects of the job you least like?

Answers to questions like these will give the interviewer quite an insight into your personality and working methods. It's obviously unrealistic to pretend everything about your job is marvellous, but you can create a very favourable impression by saying briskly something along the lines of:

- Well, I do dislike filing, but I find that if I do it as I go along so that it is never allowed to mount up, one hardly notices it.

OR:

- I really don't like stock taking very much but I've found that if the records are kept really up to date as we go along, then it doesn't present too much of a problem.

The cliché response

Probably, the most frequently asked question is, "What are you looking for in this job?" And the most frequent answer is: "A challenge". It may sound good but it doesn't say very much about you; it's more helpful to tell the interviewer what you would regard as a challenge, or say:

- I'm now actively seeking a post where I can take on increased managerial responsibilies, perhaps by joining a larger organization where the scope, and rewards will be correspondingly greater.

Levels of responsibility

Job titles vary widely from one company to another and may not necessarily be taken as a reliable guide to your functions and responsibilities. You may find yourself being asked to list your three most important responsibilities and to describe the skills, experience or other qualities required to fulfil those duties.

If your company provided training for specific functions, be sure to let your prospective employer know. If one company has seen fit to invest time and money in your training, he will take that as a measure of your competence. He will also appreciate that his own company can assume you have a certain knowledge base and future training can build on from there.

"What other areas of responsibility did you have and did your principal delegate to you?". Many people do not know how to delegate even though they may have on their staff people able to do the job better than they can. Without delegating, of course, they never find this out. Getting stuck in this sort of rut is very demotivating and a common reason for seeking job responsibilities elsewhere.

If this has been your experience, speak out and say that you are seeking a job where you will be given more scope, that you are ready and willing to take on greater responsibilities and that this is one of the reasons why you are applying for that job. Be ready to explain how exactly your present job has prepared you to take on greater responsibilities and give examples. Think about the sorts of responsibilities you particularly enjoy and which you hate. How do you go about meeting your responsibilities?

Decision-making

An important measure of responsibility lies in powers of decision-making. Your interviewer may be interested to know what sort of decisions you have been able to take alone, and which required consultation with more senior personnel. If you regularly made important decisions by yourself, you may be asked how you reached those decisions and what sort of information your decision-making was based upon. What were the results of the decisions, are there any that you regretted later, how has your experience altered your process of decision-making?

Have you ever had to take an unpopular decision? Again, this question will reflect your level of responsibility. If you have been

116

responsible for managing staff, or dealing with different departments, it may be that you have had to make a decision with quite far-reaching effects. Perhaps you had to decide to sack someone, or to declare an open-plan office a no-smoking area against the wishes of a few inveterate chain smokers. Perhaps you have had to make unpopular economies, or re-structure a department and assign people new roles and responsibilities.

Ask yourself:

- Who was affected by your decision?

- How did you communicate your decision?

- How had the situation arisen?

- Was it a quick decision or one that you had brooded about for some time?

- Were you pleased with the way you handled it?

- What did you learn from the experience and would you do it differently next time?

- Are you a decisive person?

- What kind of decisions are most difficult for you?

- Can you make decisions quickly or do you spend time in an agony of dithering?

- What happens if a decision must be made and there is no procedure to follow?

Remember, the interviewer will be just as interested in the steps you took towards making your decisions as in the decisions themselves.

Can you communicate?

In recent years, tremendous emphasis has been put on effective communication, and a whole industry has grown up on inter-personal skills. It is now realized that there is often a communication blockage within a department which is usually caused by one person. This employee either does not take the trouble to be fully informed and finds out information late — very typical of the task-oriented personality who, head down in a corner, doesn't find time to chat with colleagues. Or, this person through being busy, unaware, pre-occupied, aloof or unthinking, does not channel information. Something arrives on his or her desk and there it stays perhaps for crucial hours, days or even weeks.

There is also the office fiend who, realizing that information is power, deliberately withholds information in order to boost his own position. Being the only person in the organization who knows certain things can be a political tool in office life. Unfortunately it is frustrating for colleagues and unhealthy for the company as a whole.

Expect to be asked about your communication skills. Show that you appreciate the importance of good communication to the success of the job and that you are aware of the difficulties that can arise, especially with interdepartmental communication, and the steps that must be taken to counteract these difficulties.

- In your last job, what were your communications mainly about?

- Which means of communication did you use for different items or different people?

It may be useful for you to consider whether written or oral communication is most important to your job, and how you have used written or oral communication effectively in the past.

- Have you had to describe a complicated procedure to someone?

- How did you make sure they had understood?

- Have you had to write a proposal, an information sheet, a report, manual or handbook?

- How did you set about the task?

- Were you pleased with the result, or, looking back, could you have improved it, made it simpler, or easier to understand?

I love mankind; it's people I can't stand.

"I love meeting people" you often hear people say, but getting on with them in a working environment can be quite a different matter. It can be very exhausting especially when two large egos meet each other head on, or when there is some professional rivalry going on. The interviewer will want to know whether you can handle difficult situations with tact and diplomacy.

- Can you be understanding and sympathetic with colleagues and yet able to be tough, too, when it's called for?

- Can you motivate others, draw out the best from them and get them working with a will?

People skills play a vital part in all jobs. There is no job so high or so lowly that getting on well with people doesn't matter. If your sights are set on management, the more thought you give to these matters the more likely it is that you will be able to build an effective team when your chance to manage comes.

Give yourself some time before the interview to analyse your interpersonal skills and make notes on which areas you could work to improve. Do you have a tendency to fly off the handle, for example, and say things you later regret? Are you so shy that you put off opportunities for getting to know people?

Good people skills are a function of high self-esteem. If you are confident of your abilities and at ease with people, able to assert yourself without becoming aggressive or causing offence, then you will be able to rise above the petty office politicking that is so disruptive of good working relations. Manipulation, obstructiveness or petty backbiting should have no place in your life, whether at work or at play.

Practise good people skills at every opportunity, whether it's at work, at a party, or simply out shopping. Be courteous to

119

people at all times, and you will find life much easier to manage. Practise being assertive in a courteous way; you will find that there is no need to be rude or overbearing in order to put your ideas across. Learn to say "No" without feeling guilty; after all you are not rejecting the person, just their request. It's a very simple rule that people will respect you, if you respect them; whereas no one likes or respects someone who is loud and ill-mannered.

Working as part of a team

You may feel that you like people and get along with them just fine. But the realities of working closely together in a team with people you might not choose to have as your friends can be fraught with all manner of difficulties. Are you the sort of person who can pull a team together or do you tend to cause still further disruption by being subversive, bossy or autocratic.

The sort of questions he or she will use to evaluate your people skills may begin with a deceptively simple question or two.

- Did your last job require that you work alone unsupervised most of the time?

- How do you feel about working in a group?

- How do you perceive your role as a group member?

- Tell me about a time when you achieved something working as part of a team?

- What was your role in that team? Was that role assigned to you?

- What did you learn from that experience?

Reporting chains

This is another test of your interpersonal skills and worker/ manager relationships will reveal quite a bit about you.

120

- To whom did you report?

- Is that person one of your referees?

- Did your boss know how to get the best out of you?

- What extra responsibilities or promotion were you given?

- Who reported to you?

- How did you get the best out of them?

- When dealing with people above and below you, how do you react? Who do you feel most comfortable with?

- Who presents the most difficulties?

Your relationship with your boss

You may be asked whether you have a good relationship with your boss and whether you have discussed with him or her your desire to leave the company. This question leads up to asking you how your boss will react to the idea of your leaving. Has your boss contributed to your desire to leave and, if so, in what way? This question will be trying to probe both your manageability and your emotional maturity. It will be a question to answer diplomatically.

A prospective employer may also be curious to know how you will react if, when you come to hand in your notice, your present employer makes a move to keep you. Managers often continue with low paid staff for as long as they can get away with it. When the staff finally hand in their notice that is their cue for giving a pay rise. It's not particularly good management style in the long run, but it is widely used nevertheless.

In fact many people use a job offer from another firm as a means of negotiating from a position of strength a promotion or a higher salary in their existing place of work. It may be that they actually have no intention of moving unless certain demands are met. For this reason your motivation in applying for a new job may be tested.

Such questions may take the form of:

- Why did you apply for this job?

- What other jobs are you applying for?

- What do you hope to gain from this job?

- How well does this job fit in with your long-term plans?

- Do you have any reservations about working here?

- Is there anything you particularly like/dislike about this job?

- What will you do if your current employer tries to make you stay?

It is possible that you will be asked whether you would accept the job if it were offered to you. You may wish to counter that with another question: "Are you offering me the job?" Probably, the answer will be "No, not at this stage", but if the answer is "Yes", you should say "Yes, I am very interested in this job and I would certainly accept provided that we can agree satisfactory terms." This will bring you to the final stage of the job search: the salary negotiation. (See Chapter Eleven).

Personality and willingness

Once your qualifications and experience have been explored, what else does the interviewer have to go on? If he or she has to choose between several fairly equally-matched candidates, the interview may hinge on your personality. Also a good manager will be looking for someone who is not just willing to do the job, but who can make something of it. In short your desire to get on will be put to the test with some quite searching questions. In addition to testing your mettle, the questioner will be trying to evaluate your self-esteem, your self-starting qualities, your tenacity and your ambition.

The first question may be just that:

- Do you want to get on?

This closed question would be followed by:

- How would this job fit in with your long-term aims?

Or another set of questions:

- Do you consider yourself to be successful?

- Why?

- Where would you like to be in five years' time?

This is another old favourite to which you may have a ready answer. But this sort of question may be backed up by others testing the seriousness of your goals, the level at which you set your sights, and the realism of your aims.

Ask yourself:

- Can you demonstrate your persistence in trying to achieve your goals?

- How do you feel about your progress to date?

- Looking back, what might you have done to improve the level of your progress?

- What are your strengths?

- Your weaknesses?

- What are your greatest achievements so far?

- What gives you the most satisfaction?

- What have you done that you are most proud of?

The question, "Have you ever considered another career?" may not be the insulting question it sounds at first. You might be asked it just to test your motivation, to see whether you have given thought to all your options and are sure you are suited to the career you have in mind. Your answer should be that you have thought of other possibilities but in view of your attributes and skills you feel that this career offers you the most scope and opportunity for growth.

– Are you effective in your present position?

This is a closed question, of course, to which you will probably want to answer, "Yes". But always be prepared for closed questions to be followed up with more exacting open ones where you will have to give a good account of yourself. Such follow up questions might include:

– What steps have you taken to improve your effectiveness in your position?

– How do you evaluate competence in others?

– What do you regard as a challenge?

– What has been the biggest challenge you've had to face?

– What does a successful career mean to you?

– Has your career been successful to date?

– What has been the major influence in your career?

– Who has had the greatest effect on your career?

– Have any books influenced your business and professional life?

Can you keep your head when all about you are losing theirs?

Modern life moves very fast. That means that crises can occur and reach critical proportions very fast too. Many jobs involve meeting deadlines. In all jobs mistakes are costly. Your prospective employer will be looking for people who can demonstrate calm effectiveness in the heat of the moment. How well do you cope? Here are some questions you might be asked in order to test whether you've got grit and staying power, or whether you're the type who always runs for cover and then with hindsight, recommends all the steps that might have been taken.

- Can you think back to a time when things got out of control. What happened?

- Why had the situation occurred?

- What was your reaction?

- Did you react differently from others?

- What did you do?

- What part did you play in rescuing the situation?

- What did you learn from the experience?

- What is the most difficult situation you've ever faced?

- How had it come about?

- How did you turn it round?

- When a crisis occurs, which of your weak points/strengths come to the fore?

- Have you modified your behaviour or business practices as a result?

- What sort of situations do you find difficult?

- Why?

- Where do you turn for help?

- When has this type of situation arisen?

- How did you cope?

Working under pressure

Then there's the old chestnut, "Can you work under pressure?". The only answer to this is "yes", but that doesn't really tell the interviewer very much. All the other candidates will give the answer "yes" too. To distinguish yourself you should perhaps expand your answer with an illustration from your past when you have had to respond to a period of considerable pressure, or just make a bold statement:

 − I get a lot of satisfaction from meeting a deadline

OR:

 − It gives me a real sense of achievement to know that a customer's requirements have been met with a specially tailored system installed on schedule.

Give it some thought and make notes now: some jobs, it seems, are always stressful. Is the pressure habitual or frequent? What causes the pressure to build up — is it because of understaffing, insufficient planning, inadequate resources, rigid deadlines? Can it be avoided? How? How realistic are the remedies in terms of the budget, the cost effectiveness of the operation, the staffing levels?

Having given this question some thought, you may consider it worth while to ask at your interview what kind of pressure you would be expected to tolerate and why. It's worth knowing before you join whether the pressure in an inherent part of the job or whether it is a characteristic of that particular organization. It's often one person who can cause a blockage in the system. We've all met managers who sit on something knowing quite well that the deadline is creeping up on them. Suddenly, they make a decision: "Yes, we will have a stand at the trade fair! We need leaflets! a video! annual reports! brochures! — oh, they're out of stock. Get them reprinted PDQ! And while we're at it, let's have the catalogue redesigned!"

I worked with a managing director like this for a while; it was an incurable idiosyncrasy of his personality. When I tactfully suggested he try to make decisions earlier, he said, astonished,

"Why? I love a really good panic. It's such fun and it gets everyone working together so well!" I'm afraid it's true; many poor managers feel that the staff only really pulls together when there is a panic on. Rather than encouraging and rewarding consistent steady work and planning ahead, they prefer the excitement of a panic, regardless of the disruption caused to the rest of the business.

In some industries, creative ones particularly, there is a marked tendency to stay late even though it may not be strictly necessary. Where there are people who do not have any pressing commitments at home to get back to, it often happens that they stay drifting on at work until quite late in the evening, claiming, not unreasonably, that they can get more work done when the telephones are not ringing. The stay-late factor is complemented by the fact that these same people may not start work much before 10.00 am in the morning. If you like to keep to regular hours yourself you will need to be aware of the pressures, social and otherwise, that may be at work in certain kinds of environments.

Getting your ideas across

In addition to crises, and meeting deadlines, there is another stress factor commonly found at work. That is the situation when you feel your ideas are not getting the credit they deserve, when you or your ideas are being criticized, or when your suggestions are not being taken up. The following questions will be aimed at seeing how well your self-esteem holds up to this kind of stress.

- Do you ever have to deal with complex problems?

- Give me an example of a complex problem you've had to face.

- How did you solve it?

- Can you give me an example of a time when you had a new idea. How did you go about getting it accepted?

127

- Were you successful?

- Can you think of a time when your idea was rejected?

- Please tell me why it was rejected?

- How did you react?

- Did you try to get the idea accepted later?

- How did you set about trying to convince people?

- For what sort of things have you been most frequently criticized?

- How far is that criticism justified, do you think?

- What have you done about it?

- What is the worst criticism you have had to face?

- How did you react?

- Did you feel the criticism was emotional and personal, or rational and justified?

Time management

How you manage your time will mean the difference between success and failure in your working life. If you don't have good working habits already, set about acquiring them now. It will pay dividends in the long term in both your business and your personal life. If you are organized, and plan how you spend your time, you will achieve more. Good time management will help you with your job search too. It will transform you from a task-oriented person to a goal-oriented one, and when you have found a job you will find yourself moving into the fast lane on your way to success.

In order to manage your time effectively, you must know what you want to achieve. Everyday, set aside some time to list all your day's activities. You may find it works best to do this in the evening for the following day so that you can also mentally prepare yourself for the day ahead.

Once you have your list of things to do, prioritize them. You may think everything is urgent! But some things really are more important than others. Once you have established your priorities, stick to them and don't allow unforeseen interuptions to deflect you from your tasks. At the end of the day, review your progress and prepare your list of priorities for the following day.

These are some questions that you may be asked at an interview. The questioner will be trying to find out whether you are a clock-watcher, a workaholic, or an effective time-manager.

- How many projects/tasks do you usually have to handle at any one time?

- Is this too many, do you think?

- Can you manage your time well?

- Could you describe a typical day for me, please?

- Do you plan your day?

- How do you set about it?

- How do you divide your time between your various tasks?

- How do you organize yourself to ensure you get things done on time?

- What problems do you encounter in getting things done?

- Have you got a method or system of working?

- How does it work?

- What happens to your system if a crisis occurs?

- Can you tell me about an emergency which caused you to rethink/reschedule/restructure your work?

- How many hours a week do you work on average?

- Do you often work late to finish your tasks?

- Do you take work home? Ever? Often?

- How do you feel about your present workload?

- If you have to work under pressure for a long period of time, what sustains you?

- How do you maintain your enthusiasm?

- How do you maintain the enthusiasm of others?

- How do you keep up your energy levels?

- Can you give me an example of such a time? Please tell me what happened.

- How did you react afterwards?

What to do if the interviewer does all the talking

In an ideal interview situation, you should get to do about 80 per cent of the talking. Many people have poor listening ability. This does not mean they are deaf. It may be that the person interviewing you has always prided himself on his leadership qualities. He has good verbal skills and is accustomed to dominating a discussion. Some people always prefer the known to the unknown: the company and his experience within it is known; you, the applicant, are not. If the interviewer is nervous or inexperienced he may do rather more of the talking than he should leaving you wondering how to get a word in edgeways.

A good interview should take the form of a dialogue and if the dialogue doesn't develop you may have to take the initiative. For the simple fact is that while the interviewer is talking he cannot be finding out anything about you. It is true that he will probably be making the same mistake with all the candidates. But if you are successful in getting across something positive about yourself you will be that much more memorable to him than someone who fails. Suppose the interviewer is rambling on about the company, how long they have been in that building, the history of the firm, his history with the company, where he lives and so on and on, you may have to start to interrupt to get your point across.

One strategy is to ask how long your interviewer has available for the interview. This will act as a gentle prompt for him to get on with it, or you could say:

- I am extremely interested in this but I'm afraid I am expected back at work in an hour's time. I expect there are quite a few things you would like to ask me in the time that's left.

OR:

- I have another appointment at twelve o'clock. I am anxious not to leave before I have had a chance to tell you why I think my experience is relevant to this post.

If this does not work say simply:

- May I tell you a bit about myself now?

OR:

- I wonder if I could tell you a bit about my experience and why I think I could do this job.

Other ploys are:

- It might be helpful to you if I told you how I handled a similiar project in the past?

- Do you need to know my strengths in this particular field?

- Would you like more details about my time at XYZ?

- Perhaps I should tell you how my experience fits in here.

If the interviewer seems to be winding up the interview and you feel some vital areas of your experience have not been covered, you could slip in something like:

- There is just one more thing. I think I should tell you about my marketing experience with ABC. It really is extremely relevant to the post you have on offer.

Or put the interviewer under a bit of pressure by saying:

- Do you feel confident about my ability to do this job? Is there anything else you would like to know about me?

OR:

- Do you have any doubts about my ability to do this job?

If the interviewer indicates that he is satisfied you could say:

- Good. I can expect to hear favourably from you soon then?

After all, if the interviewer has no doubts about your ability to do the job, he is bound to offer you the job, isn't he?

Interviewing for a management position

If you have been taking your career seriously, sooner than later you will have to go for a management position. You may be promoted within your present firm, but in some ways it will be easier for you to assume the mantle of management in a new company. It's a good reason to move, but you may find it presents you with one of the toughest interviews you will ever have to face. Once you have made the transition your subsequent job moves will be easier so you may prefer to achieve management status in your present job before moving on. However, an internal promotion will inevitably create difficulties with your former fellow workers, some of whom may have been striving for your new managerial status themselves. It is a risk that the promotion may not be taken seriously by your erstwhile fellows who may be resentful or mischievous in their dealings with you, especially difficult if you are supposed to be managing them. It will take tact, imagination and diplomacy to stay on good terms — a good test of your management skills. Do not be surprised if your colleagues try to see how much they can get away with, provoking you to make choices between friendship and your career status. Starting a managerial post in a new company may be much easier for you in so far as your subordinates will see you as a manager from the beginning and it will be easier to establish your authority with people who have not known you as a chum for many years.

The word "management" means different things to different people. Often people say "managed" when they mean "supervised". If you are responsible for a team of people while they are working on a particular problem — competitor analysis, for example, or distribution strategies — then you have supervisory responsibility for that team for the duration of that project. It is true that motivating people, keeping them enthusiastic and producing results on schedule, is a management function. But unless you hold fiscal responsibilities, including the hiring, firing and salary reviews of employees, you are not truly a manager. These distinctions may seem pedantic, but at an interview questions probably will be asked about your responsibilities and it will be helpful for you to know their implications.

These questions may include:

- Tell me, what do you understand by the term "management"?

- How many people do you manage?

- Tell me about the people you manage. What positions do they hold? What are their duties?

- Who holds responsibility for hiring and firing these people?

- Do you conduct regular job appraisals and salary reviews on these people?

- Have you ever fired anyone?

- How many people have you had to fire?

- For what reasons did you fire them?

- Were any of the people you have fired originally recruited by you?

- What do you think went wrong?

133

- How many appointments have you made?

- How did you set about making those appointments?

Now that your prospective employer has satisfied himself about whether you are a manager or a supervisor, he or she will probably move on to ask you about your team-building capabilities. These questions may include some of the following:

- How do you communicate with your staff?

- How do you set about getting new employees up to speed?

- How much attention do you pay to training?

- What training techniques do you use?

- How do you pull a team together?

- How do you motivate the team?

- How do you deal with people who are obstructive of the team's efforts?

- How do you build morale?

- What are the weak points in your team?

- How did you arrive at a structure for your team?

- How do you set about determining job objectives?

- How does your team report to you?

- How do you reward your team?

CHAPTER NINE

What you Need to Know

Most organizations are waking up to the fact that they have to be open and forthcoming about themselves if they are to attract good people to work for them. Human resources are valuable. In fact, people are the most valuable resource a company has. The days of "mushroom management" — keep people in the dark, shovel them dirt, and expect miracles to happen overnight — are, fortunately, over. Loosening hierachical structures and a more open management style involves an acceptance of new values, such as:

- trusting people
- sharing information
- sharing power
- sharing decision-making
- taking account of people's feelings
- taking acount of people's opinions
- seeing people as more than a job description
- accommodating differing points of view
- considering people's needs and expectations

All this means that a company with a sensible approach to recruitment will be seeking to find out how far an applicant's values and aspirations are compatible with its own. To do this it will have to be honest about itself and its expectations. It is also important for you to know and understand the company's objectives. Companies like and reward loyal staff and it is that much easier to be loyal if you can respect and identify with the company's aims.

The company should try to explain to you what the job is about; to this end they may show you, either as a paper document or perhaps as a video, case-studies of people who have recently joined and the work that they do. Sometimes companies will actually arrange for you to meet some of the staff so that you can ask about the disadvantages of the job as well as the good things and this should take the form of a private conversation. It is not an interview and confidences from both sides should be respected. J. Sainsbury's, and other companies with a rather innovative and enlightened approach to recruitment, allow people to try job-sample exercises to see what the job is like. Another method is to give an applicant several statements about the job and to ask whether the applicant thinks they are true or false. This can identify areas where expectations differ considerably from the job on offer. For example, an applicant may be asked whether it is true or false that the job involves a high degree of communication with the public, or calls for computer knowledge or detailed checking skills.

If you go to an interview at a company which does not have any particular policy for allowing candidates to find out about the jobs they are applying for, why not ask whether you could spend an afternoon at the firm seeing what the job involves? If you have not had a job before, or have had a long interval betweeen jobs, this is a good way of finding out what kinds of activity you will be called upon to do. It will also help you to feel more at ease on your first day if you can visualize where you will sit and what your colleagues will be like.

The firm may feel that it is being very open and co-operative by giving you a detailed job description, but unless you have done something similiar before, a list of tasks and responsibilities does not tell you how you are to carry them out, nor will you necessarily know how to prioritize those tasks.

Role ambiguity is one of the biggest sources of dissatisfaction at work. Uncertainty about the expectations of others about one's decision making powers and the limits of one's responsibilities, especially when combined with a lack of proper evaluation and commitment to advancement, can devastate sensitive but concientious hard-workers. Try and find out as much as possible about your role. To whom will you report? Is that the same as the person who is interviewing you? A job description may tell you that you will report to the Production Manager, but leave out the other people in the department who may also be expecting to have feedback from you. Does reporting to a person also mean that you can expect training, supervision, support and orientation from that person? What happens if the Production Manager is frequently away from the office seeing suppliers? Will it mean that both reporting and supervision are suspended and that the new job holder will have to simply sink or swim until the Production Manager hoves into view again? Does anyone report to you? How many people? What level of supervision or training or monitoring are they to expect from you?

Is there a training period and if so who is training you and in what? Is there a probationary period? How long does it last and what is being monitored during this period?

Where can you go within the organization? Is it possible to move within the company? What procedures are there for moving people around? Is there a logical progression from your present job to the next rung of the ladder?

What about the location? Is the company you are about to join going to stay put, or is the lease about to run out? Are there plans to relocate to a greenfield site or to move into a city centre? What will be the implications for you and the amount of travelling you will have to do if they move?

What is the company really like? Is it stable? Is it growing? Are its products becoming obsolete or is innovation the key to its success? Does it pride itself on staying ahead of the field in terms of new product, new design, or ecological awareness? Does it have a corporate vision? Is it committed to a cause? Does it care about ecological issues, or the local community? Does it have a policy about training, internal promotion, child care, job sharing? Are its values old-fashioned and patriarchal, modern but macho, or a caring co-operative with power and influence shared amongst its membership of expert individualists? Are there women at the top? How many? And are they at the real top or only at the glass ceiling?

What is the company set to become? Where are its values and corporate structures leading it? Or is there someone powerful and dynamic at the top who is steering the ship his way and cares little about what anyone else thinks.

It is helpful to know how your performance will be monitored and what feedback will be given. Many organizations have appraisal schemes now, but too little time is allocated to carrying them out thoroughly and the forms that are used tend to go out of date quite quickly, not really reflecting the most up-to-date development of the job.

All jobs develop in some way. Try to find out what circumstances led to the creation of the job you are now applying for. If you are replacing someone who has already left, find out how recently that person left. A job that has been vacant for a while is tough assignment to fill, especially if it is a management position. People who are supposed to report to you will have lost the habit of doing so. By now they will be used to a considerable amount of authority and autononomy and may resent a newcomer to the point of outright hostility. You should also try to find out whether the job you are taking on is exactly the same as that held by the out-going post-holder, or whether it has been modified in some way. Find out also whether anyone else has left at the same time. As a result of streamlining, it is not unusual for companies to try to re-design jobs so that two people are replaced with one. How successfully this works out depends very much on the thought and planning that has gone into the new structure and the calibre of the in-coming candidate.

Warning signs

It will be useful to you to ask about the turnover of staff. You should not be surprised to find that throughout the company several people have left or plan to leave the company. If it is a large organization with several tiers of employment you can expect a high level of turnover, especially at the lower end of the scale. What is more worrying to the new employee is a cluster of resignations at the middle or upper levels of management. This is generally a symptom of a breakdown in communications, weakness in the fabric of the company, or a disagreement over policies. It can create a dramatic lowering of morale amongst the remaining staff. Full recovery of the firm on to stable ground could take a year or two. If the company is a wholly-owned subsidiary of a larger company, and you are considering a management post, you should perhaps investigate the level of commitment the parent company has to the smaller company. If you think the company could be wobbly, but you still want to proceed with the job, you may wish to negotiate yourself a contract with a six-month, or even a year's, notice period.

Closing the interview

The interviewer will bring the interview to a close; it is his prerogative to take the initiative here. If your application has not been successful, then you will probably receive a letter letting you down. Occasionally you will be told at the interview, in which case it is unlikely to come as a surprise. It will have become apparent during the interview that you and the job are not a good fit and the interviewer will perhaps take the view that it will be fairer to you to let you know definitely sooner rather than later. In this case, he may say something like this:

- Thank you very much indeed for coming to see us today and giving us your time. You have a number of strong points, but this is a demanding job and I think it is fair to say that you simply don't have the level of marketing and sales experience we need for this particular post. We will have other openings coming up in the near future which may be a closer match with your skills and experience and if you would like us to consider you for those, we will be happy to keep your name on file for consideration at a later date.

However, it is more likely that you will have to wait for the outcome of the interview, especially if this is the first of a series of interviews. The interviewer will probably say something like this:

- Thank you very much indeed for coming along. I am sure you can appreciate that we have had a very good response to our advertisement and I still have a number of candidates to see. I should complete this first round of interviews by the middle of next week. We will then draw up a shortlist for people to come back and see us again for a second interview. We have your address and telephone number — we'll be in touch by the end of next week. If you think of anything more you want to know, please don't hesitate to ring me.

It is quite a good idea to confirm that you expect to hear by the end of next week and that you would like to ring the following Monday if you still have not heard. Probably the interviewer will respect you for wanting to keep up a certain level of initiative in your application.

CHAPTER TEN

Following up an Interview

Briefly review the interview. Make sure you have a note of the names and positions of all the people you met. It will be embarrassing (and lose you points) if you meet them again at a second interview and can't remember their names. Write some short notes about your impressions of the company — did it seem a cheerful place to work, were people welcoming, was the interview professional. Note down before you forget any items of interest that you were told — numbers of employees, turnover, new product lines and so on. Think about whether you could see yourself fitting in there. How did the interview go? Note down anything you did not know and resolve to find out about it in preparation for the second interview. If you feel you said or did something unwise, think about how you could make a more favourable impression next time. Once you have a strategy for getting it right next time, leave the problem. Don't dwell on it or allow it to keep you awake at night. Keep in mind all the positive things you did:

- you wore the right clothes; you looked professional

- you were punctual

- you looked confident, your posture was good; your body language told the right story

- you listened to the questions

- you spoke up for your abilities

- you showed you were knowledgeable about the business

- you found out what you wanted to know

- you made a positive impression

What else can you do?

There is one more thing. When you get home, write a short note to the person who has interviewed you. Thank him for giving you his time and use the opportunity to reiterate how well your skills match the job and how interested you are in working for the company. If you met more than one person at the interview, mention that person by name too. Say something like this:

Dear Mr Rose

It was a great pleasure to meet you and Ms Brownlow today. Thank you for giving up so much of your time to discuss the job in detail and to show me around the office and warehouse.

My four years with Blanks in consumer marketing has given me the opportunity to learn a great deal about the planning and co-ordination of development strategy, including budgeting, purchasing and supplier liaison.

I feel that my skills and experience are extremely relevant to the post of Marketing Manager. I look forward to hearing from you.

Yours sincerely

Pamela Pyke

Make sure your letter is correctly spelt, immaculately presented and delivered the next day. It should be short and confident. The letter will focus attention on your application again and should create an extremely positive impression by reinforcing the points you have already made in your interview. If you get home kicking yourself because there was something important you forgot to say in the interview, use the thank you letter as an opportunity to fill in the gap.

It is worth writing, even if you have lost interest in this particular job altogether. Don't overlook the importance of networking. Having been interviewed, you have made a contact in the world of work, and in the career or field of your choice. That person has contacts, too; probably many contacts, so don't hesitate to ask the interviewer to keep you in mind if they hear of any other opportunities that might be suitable for you. If you have established a bit of a rapport with the interviewer, and that person moves on to a different company, you will have expanded your network of contacts again.

Do not ask any further questions in your letter as that may be taken to indicate hesitancy on your part and will weaken the positive impression you are trying to create.

If there are things you want to know, by all means telephone a day or two later. If the date has come and gone by which you expected to hear from the company, ringing up with a further question is a good opportunity to enquire also about the status of your application.

The second interview

This is usually with a different — and more senior — person than the first person who interviewed you and it will generally be more "in depth", probing your skills, attributes and motivations. It is not at all unusual for people who have sailed through the first interview to flunk the second. The reason is generally nerves so boost your morale and keep up your self-confidence. Remember preparation is the key to success.

What the company will want to ask your referees

References will not normally be sought until the interviews are complete; in fact you may be offered the job straightaway subject to satisfactory references. In order to obtain a quick response, references are very often sought by telephone. You will, of course, have checked with your referees and secured their agreement. If you have had the same referees for several years, it is courteous to ring them and tell them that you are now looking for a new job so they are aware that they may be contacted.

The interviewer will telephone your referee and introduce him- or herself, tell them a bit about the organization and the sort of tasks you will be called upon to do. The interviewer will then try to establish your working and reporting relationship with the referee and ask for their reactions to the job as outlined.

For example, the interviewer may say:

- Good morning. My name is Alex Dunkley. I am the Product Group Manager with Sanders. Peter Stewart gave me your name as a reference. We are considering Peter for the post of Assistant Product Manager and I am ringing you to ask if you have a few moments to give us your reactions to Peter's work with you at Jiggers. I understand from Peter that you were his immediate boss and that he reported directly to you. Is that correct? Can you give me some idea of Peter's main responsibilities?

- We will be asking our new recruit to assist with the launch of a new upholstery fabric and we will need someone with some promotional experience. I understand Peter was involved with a similar project at Jiggers. Can you tell me a bit about that?

- Peter gave us the impression of being very creative with a great deal of flair in putting together point of sale materials. But we rather suspected his administration skills may be a bit weak. Do you think that is a fair assessment?

The interviewer may ask what kind of duties you undertook when employed by your referee and what strengths and weaknesses you showed in those circumstances. He may point out some of the differences between his organization and the referee's company, and ask how the referee thinks you will react to the different environment. Your referee may be asked to think back to when he or she first employed you, and recall how long after being hired you felt confident on the job. He will want to know how you got on with your colleagues, clients or customers.

He may make some observation about you and ask whether your referee thinks it is genuinely characteristic of you or something that was likely to be due to nervousness or stress during the interview. For example, he may say:

- We all liked Peter. He seemed very friendly and person-able, but we felt he was rather shy. This job will involve a certain amount of marketing. How do you think he will cope?

The classic question when the referee will feel really put on the spot is:

- Looking back over the two years that Peter was with you, would you hire him again?

Then, depending on the answer and whether he wants to probe more carefully, he may say:

- Can you tell me why you feel that way?

The interviewer will then say something like:

- Thank you very much indeed for giving me so much of your time. I very much appreciate having a chance to talk to you and I think it has been very useful in helping me to understand Peter better. Is there anything else you think I should know before I make a decision?

Usually the interviewer will then leave his telephone number and ask the referee to call him if he thinks of anything else that may be useful and ring off.

CHAPTER ELEVEN

Negotiating your Salary

Your salary should not come up for discussion until you have received a job offer. Once the firm has committed itself, you will be in a much stronger negotiating position. In fact, the roles are reversed — you are the chosen candidate and thus become the buyer. The potential employer has become the seller.

Some people are afraid to negotiate a salary because they fear they may lose the job offer altogether. In fact, it will demonstrate your poise, confidence, and self-esteem. Your new employer will see that you value yourself and know the value of your skills and experience. It will also demonstrate your negotiating skills, which your employer will be glad to see. However, there is no need to negotiate your salary just for the sake of it. If the company suggests a figure beyond your wildest dreams, all you need say is "Thank you, that would be acceptable".

Always keep your negotiations pleasant and positive. They should be conducted in a tone of sweet reasonableness, emphasizing the worth of the job and your particular strengths for that job. Any aggression on your part would be completely misplaced and may well lead to the job offer being withdrawn.

It is important to negotiate the highest salary you possibly can because all salary reviews will be built on it and also because other items, — maternity pay, for example, sickness pay or redundancy payments, will be based on your salary. It is also true, however, that the more you are paid, the more the company will expect from you.

Your salary should be paid on the basis of the importance and worth of the post. Your new position may be similiar to your present or previous job, but it is not the same. Therefore, your old salary is not relevant to the new position and should not be used as a basis for negotiation. For that reason, try to keep your present or past earnings to yourself. However, if you are backed into a corner and have to reveal your earnings, say something like this:

- In my present/last position I am/was earning in excess of £_____ . However I expect to improve considerably on that because this particular position involves greater responsibility.

It is often the case that the employer will ask what salary you would like. Obviously the company doesn't have an unlimited budget. Your salary will have to fall in line with comparable jobs across the industry and with employees doing similiar jobs within that company. You should try to get the employer to show his hand first. Say something like this:

- I expect you have a salary range for this post. Can you give me an indication of what that range is?

The difference in salaries in a range may vary by up to £5,000 or more, so it's important to follow up quickly with some statement re-affirming your particular skills for the job and claiming a salary at the higher end of the range. For example, say:

- In view of my particular strengths [list them, management training, administration skills and knowledge of on-line data retrieval or whatever] I would expect to be near the top of that range.

Keep the salary negotiations on the worth of the job. It is possible that the potential employer will ask what you need, but a salary should never be negotiated from need. If you are asked this, turn it round straight away to job worth again. Don't say: "I need £_____," but instead you should say something like this:

- I gather from my contacts with other companies in this industry that comparable positions are paid from £_____ to £_____ . In view of my extensive experience of [sales/ managment/ administration etc.], I would expect to be at the top of that range.

Your prospective employer wants to employ you and you have been selected from a shortlist of several other candidates, so you should be in a strong position to negotiate your terms. However, the employer will be under pressure from the company to keep salary payments within budget. He or she may not have the authority to exceed a certain salary limit. If you are asked for the minimum salary you will accept, say:

- From our conversations I understand that this position is a demanding one. I am prepared to give much more than a minimum level of effort. In view of the fact that you are looking for maximum effort from me from day one, I am surprised to be asked to consider starting at a minimum level of remuneration.

At this point the employer will have to commit to a figure and say:

- The most I can offer you at the present time is £_____ .

You can look disappointed as you say:

- I see. I had expected rather more than that. I thought that, in view of the importance of this post, it would pay £_____ [name a figure at least £2,000 higher than the one you have just been quoted].

Your prospective employer may then say:

- I'm sorry, but £_____ is the most I can offer.

In this case, you can ask about other benefits and pay reviews. Say:

- That's very disappointing. If I were to accept your salary offer, perhaps you could give me some idea about how soon I could expect a review.

Salary reviews are usually carried out at certain specified intervals according to company policy, and the employer may have little if any discretion over the matter. However, it is certainly worth asking as you may be able to negotiate for a salary review after six months rather than in a year's time. Go on to ask about other benefits:

What other benefits does the company offer? Do they provide luncheon vouchers/a car/share option scheme/pension scheme/bonus scheme/membership of a private medical care scheme/subsidised mortgage/re-location expenses?

Perks and fringe benefits are not ideal. They are payments in kind rather than payments in cash, and cash is often preferable in so far as you can spend it as you want. Remember that if perks were converted into cash and added on to your salary, then:

a) your salary would be higher
b) the items that will be based on your salary — bonuses, holdiay pay, sick pay, maternity pay, pensions and overtime — would be correspondingly higher also.

Never accept the offer at the time it is made. Tell the employer you would like to think about it and ask for plenty of time. Say something like this:

- Thank you for the offer and for explaining the financial position to me. I would like to have the offer in writing and I would like to think about it, if I may. I could give you a definite decision by the middle of next week. Would that be acceptable?

It is very unlikely that a week will be acceptable, but try to get as much time as possible. The employer will say that he has other people waiting to hear from him and that he is under an obligation to let them know what the situation is by the day after tomorrow. He will put pressure on you to decide within 24 hours. The longer you can delay making a decision, the more likely it is that:

a) you may get a better offer from the company
b) you may get a better offer from somewhere else
c) other candidates will be kept waiting and may lose interest or accept other offers.

If the company begins to feel it has fewer choices, it will feel under pressure and may improve its offer. Once you have agreed a time by which to let the company have your decision, however, you must contact them promptly and without fail. If you delay, the prospective employer may well feel justified in making an offer to someone else.

There may be times in your life when it is worth accepting a job offer even if it does not pay particularly well. If this is your first job, you may feel that it is better to gain some experience and build up your qualifications, even if the pay is less than you would like. It may be that the firm offers special training, prospects of accelerated promotion or unusual job experience, and these things may ultimately matter more to your career than short-term rewards. If you have found it hard to find a job and have been repeatedly turned down you may feel so relieved to have been offered a job at all that you won't feel like pushing your luck. Only you are in a position to know what the job is worth to you and evaluate your prospects accordingly. However, it is unlikely to harm your relationship with the company if you negotiate the best deal you can for yourself and it will enhance your self-esteem.

The firm recruiting you may be pleased if you ask for more money; if you can look after your own interests it will encourage them to think that you will look after the company's interests too. If you can't or won't seek out the best deal for yourself you may not be the best person to take on fiscal or management responsibilities with the firm. You may think a few hundred a year doesn't make that much difference, but over a few years, that will amount to a considerable sum especially as increments and other perks will be based on the salary you initially agreed.

CHAPTER TWELVE

Power to the Women

If you are planning to return to work after a long interval, you will probably need to conduct a job search in a very strategic fashion. The first thing to do is to put your networking skills into action. Let it be widely known amongst your friends and acquaintances that you are looking for an interesting new job. Make sure they know what sort of experience of work you have had, what skills you can offer and what sort of work you would like. Contacts are a very good way of finding jobs and, in fact, 50 per cent of jobs in this country are found in this way, so you cannot afford to ignore such a very promising source of work. Hone up your c.v., have it beautifully typed or wordprocessed and then photocopy it. Have it ready so that when a friend of a friend comes up with a lead, you can act quickly to send it off with a letter of application.

As a gesture of seriousness about your job search, you may find it a good idea to change your appearance in some way. A new hairstyle, or the loss of a few pounds will boost your morale. A change in your appearance is a clear signal to your friends that you want to start something new and embark on a new phase of life. It will also help you to start programming yourself to think like a successful career woman so that you won't be caught out at interviews by your old housewifely self who perhaps feels rather unsure of herself.

Career counselling is free from your local Jobcentre or Employment Office, and you can make use of their services whether you are employed or not. But ultimately you know more about yourself and what you want than even the best-trained professional.

If you have a fairly clear idea of what you would like to do, but don't know whether your qualifications are suitable, or want information about further training, ask at the local Jobcentre or consult the careers section of your local public library.

Many professions now have active women's groups who will give you advice, help and support. Some of them even run their own training courses. Write to them for information but, please, do remember to enclose a stamped addressed envelope. Most of these organizations are self-help groups and, whilst they're keen to help, they don't have a big budget to do so.

There is now a big drive to get women into careers where women are traditionally under-represented and training of all kinds is now available to women more readily than ever before. You may find a courses in management, economics, or information technology and computing available at the nearest polytechnic, or college of further education.

The housewife and mother returning to work is all too likely to slip into an under-stimulating dead end job because either she fails to make the most of the skills and abilities she has, or fails to realize that even a very short course can dramatically expand the range of work you can apply for.

Also valuable are the many courses now available in public speaking, self-assertiveness and confidence building. In fact, coming through an interview with flying colours and a job offer has a great deal to do with confidence. Start boosting yours now; don't wait until the invitations to interview arrive. Only continuous practice will bring about long-term change and rewards.

It is important for your self-confidence to realize that home-based skills can be every bit as demanding and valuable as work-based ones. Every home-maker and mother is a manager and an organizer. She routinely takes important decisions on family finances, resources, and people management. She meets deadlines and manages a budget as a matter of course.

Have you ever put on a play, completed a course of study, raised money for charity, or learnt a new skill? If you can say yes to any of these you have demonstrated, however unknowingly at the time, a goal-oriented approach to problem-solving involving method, application, and persistence. These are valuable qualities in the workplace. Put everything down on your c.v.. If you organized a barn dance to raise money for the local church whilst running a family at home and brushing up your French, your prospective employer should know. If you play sports, put them down, together with any tournaments you've won; if you have languages, or a facility for writing or music, make the most of it on your c.v..

While you're looking for work the value of voluntary work should not be under-estimated. In fact, if your financial position permits your taking on unpaid work, you may well find voluntary work exploits your talents in a very special and satisfying way. At all events, voluntary work, whether it's working on committees, or fund raising, or helping to run a community newsletter, will give you a good grounding in organization, administration and interpersonal skills — excellent preparation for returning to work.

When you make your application, say why you want to return to work, and emphasize that you fully intend to build a career for yourself, now that children are no longer tying you to the home.

Keep your application positive and upbeat in tone. Only use positive statements and don't be apologetic. Never set up a relative comparison by using words like "although". "Although" is known as a concessive conjunction; you must make no concessions! If you feel tempted to start a sentence with "although I haven't done this, I have done that", just concentrate on the last half of the sentence.

NOT

- Although I have been out of work for six years, I have been working with a community project for the last eighteen months.

BUT

- For the last eighteen months, I have been working with a community project, helping to organize transport for disabled people, and this has given me valuable organizational and communications skills.

NOT

- Although my shorthand is a little rusty, I can still type at 60 wpm.

BUT

- I can offer some shorthand and typing, with a typing speed of 60 wpm.

Once you've got a job, keep working at your career. You may feel very nice and cosy where you are and moving on may seem very threatening. But think, you may have to work for many, many more years yet. Do you still want to be doing this job in three years' time? in five? in ten?

Aim to do the job you have to the very best of your ability, but always think about your next step. Set yourself a time limit for making your next move. Take on as much administrative work as you can and concentrate on figures. Someone who can read a balance sheet, use statistics, understand cash flow and keep to a tight budget is going to increase her value to the company and put herself in the fast lane for promotion. The more you understand about the way the company works and makes its profits, the less likely you are to get stuck in a dead end position. This is frequently what happens to even the most able women. Because Julia proves herself to be the most superbly competent secretary or sales administration assistant the firm has ever had, she is likely to remain there. ("How will we ever find another Julia?") What Julia needs to demonstrate is that she has reserves of talent the firm has only just begun to tap, and that if she can be invaluable as a secretary, then how much more valuable she will be as a manager.

Moving on to higher things. . .

If you are an ambitious secretary, chafing at the bit to get away from the grind of shorthand and typing and longing for more responsibility, you may want to say that you feel your strengths as an administrator are the most valuable and, say, organizing the company's annual sales conference, staff training, or whatever gives you the most satisfaction. In an interview, be prepared to answer what is the most irksome part of your work, too, and why you want to change.

Phrase your answer carefully and diplomatically, focusing on the positive aspects of the new job. The utterly maddening foibles of your present employer are not likely to be of interest to anyone but yourself, and a prospective employer will respect your loyalty in not allowing yourself to get drawn in to making any personal criticism of your present principal.

Explore carefully just what opportunities there might be for you to get your teeth into other responsibilities. Your prospective employer may be genuinely relieved to delegate as much as possible to you. But whether or not there is a will to give you extra responsibilities, the reality of the work load may mean that you are chained to your typewriter or wordprocessor much more than you would wish.

If your principal is sincerely interested in your taking on other tasks, it is reasonable to expect some assistance to keep the secretarial work at manageable levels. If your principal is not amenable to this, then the secretarial function may come to dominate your life anyway. Clarification of this early on in the relationship may save a lot of frustration later on.

To get ahead, you must make it clear to your company that you want to get on, that you want training, that you are hungry for opportunities, and ready for to take on new responsibilities. Find out all you can about the company you work for and ask questions with a view to taking the next step on the promotion ladder.

CHAPTER THIRTEEN

Setting your Sights if you are Disabled

All the advice in this book about preparation and self-confidence applies just as much to the disabled as to the more fortunate. An employer will be impressed if you have found out as much as you can about his business and if you have also thought about your own strengths and skills.

You probably know that firms employing more than twenty people have a legal duty to employ a quota of registered disabled people, so they may be really pleased to see you. If you tell them of your disability when you apply for jobs, you can help them to satisfy their quotas. Try to explain your disability as simply and truthfully as possible; many people will not understand the medical terminology. You may have to initiate the discussion about your disability, especially if it is a hidden disability, because the interviewer may be afraid to ask you. But only do this once you have told the employer what you can do. And when you do come round to explaining your disability tell him about your strategies for overcoming your difficulties. If you are turned down for a job, always find out why. Remember not to take the rejection personally; able-bodied people will have been turned down too. If an employer says, "I'd like to hire you, but. . ." try to find out what is really worrying him. Explain that as a disabled person, you have developed a certain creativity about problem-solving; if, amongst the range of tasks you have to perform, there is one task that might create a problem, say: "Give me a day or two and I think I might come up with a solution to that one". Or maybe you could swop that particular task with someone else and take on something that he normally does but which you could easily do.

If you apply for a job you have done before, you will be in a good position to convince a new employer that you can do it. If you are applying for something new, you should try to find out as much as you can about that job so that you can reassure yourself and your prospective employer about your ability to carry it out. It may be necessary to use some special equipment, but much of this can be had on a free loan so it need not be a financial worry to either you or your employer. Find out as much as you can about what you need and what is available and from whom so that you can forestall these objections.

Do you need special facilities for attending an interview? Ring up as soon as an interview has been arranged and explain your needs: a nearby car parking space or wheelchair access, for example. Let the person who will be interviewing you know if you wish to be accompanied by an interpreter or helper.

The person interviewing you may not know very much about the condition you have or how it will affect your work. You should try to talk about it using simple language; a long and complicated medical history may not be very helpful. All they will want to know is whether you can do the job and what equipment or special facilities you will need to do it. It's best to be completely open and honest about any difficulties you face and the special equipment you may need. Most employers will feel reassured by being put fully in the picture, and they will respect your honesty. They may become nervous if they feel that you are trying to hide your difficulties from them.

Help at hand

There are special tools and pieces of equipment which you can have on a free loan which may help you at work. These include special loud speaking telephone aids for those with hearing disabilities, and special chairs and wheel-chairs for those with mobility difficulties. There are devices which enlarge the print on computer screens and voice synthesizers which can help you with computers.

Travel grants are available if you cannot use public transport or if public transport routes do not go past the place of work.

Employers may be interested to know that grants are available to them to modify or improve their premises to accommodate the needs of the disabled.

Employers may not know about all these things and will be grateful for the information. Research the help that is available to you so that you can present your case in a positive way. Jobcentres and Jobclubs will have the answers. Also contact any organizations or societies that have a particular interest in your disability.

You are valuable

In the end, it is your qualifications, work experience, enthusiasm, knowledge, self-confidence and positive approach that will persuade the prospective employer to hire you. Once you have explained your disability, move the conversation on to your skills and attributes.

Coping with a disability demonstrates:

- resilience

- determination

- courage

- motivation

- commitment

- energy

Many fit and able-bodied people don't possess these qualities, so you should feel confident that you have something very special to offer.

Set your sights and target an organization in your locality. Read up about that area of business and find out all you can about it. If you can show that you know a good deal about the employer's business, his markets, products, special features, and competitors, he will be keen to hire you. Familiarize yourself

158

with the company report and master the facts and figures involved. If you apply for a particular job that you have seen advertised, and they turn you down, don't give up: ask if there is something else you can do. Jobs are evolving and developing all the time and new jobs are constantly being created. Try saying "these are my skills, this is what I know, these are the things I can do and this is what I think I can achieve" — and ask for a trial period so that you can prove your abilities.

CHAPTER FOURTEEN

The First Day at Work

Congratulations on your success! You put together the c.v. that led to an interview which you passed with flying colours. Now you're facing the first day at work and if it's your first job or the first job in a long while, it will seem intimidating. What was the secret of your interview success? You prepared yourself for it and you built up your self-confidence. Now you must prepare yourself for the first day of work so that you can continue to make a good impression.

You will be glad to know that one of the first things you will be asked about on your first day is how you are going to be paid. Your employer will need your P45, the name, address and sorting code of your bank, and your bank account number. Make sure you have these handy. You may also need to supply the name and address of your family doctor and nearest of kin in case of illness or accident at work.

One thing that will help ease the strain of the first few weeks, is to have stocked up sensibly on household and personal items. Make sure the freezer is stocked up with some basic items like bread and butter and a few meals which can be quickly heated up from frozen. Stock up the storecupboard with tins of soup, tomatoes, rice, pasta, and beans, tuna fish, and pâté. You really may not feel like doing much cooking when you come home from work — at least to begin with — but you will still need nourishing food. It will help if you know you can quickly rustle up something without too much bother and without last minute shopping. Remember too that things like eggs and fruit are nature's fast foods and very nourishing. Dried milk is handy to have in case you run out of milk, and do make sure you have some bouillon cubes, Bovril or Marmite to hand. These can make delicious sustaining drinks on those evenings when you just feel like flopping into bed without bothering to eat.

You will save yourself a good deal of trouble too if you are confident that you have sufficient washing-up liquid, washing powder, toilet rolls and other basic household items to tide you over for at least a couple of weeks.

When you've been at home where jeans and sweaters will see you through for most of the time, you may find the need to appear reasonably smart for work takes a bit of organizing at first. Make sure you have two or three pairs of smart, comfortable shoes to hand and that they are clean and not in need of a cobbler's attention. Men will need to stock up on clean, holeless socks; women should buy several pairs of tights to see them through the first week or two.

Plan your clothes for the first week so that you have clean shirts, underwear and accessories ready to hand. If you are not sure what to wear, keep it simple and classic. Now is NOT the time to buy a whole new wardrobe. It's easy to buy a stunning outfit that is too dressy for daily office wear and feeling over-dressed at work will not improve your confidence. Wait until you can assess the kind of clothes you will need everyday and in the meantime wear a classic suit or well cut, well co-ordinated separates — clothes you can forget about and won't have to fuss with. Do make sure you can control your temperature though. If it is summer, the air conditioning may be set too cold; have by you a cardigan, light jacket or sweater. In winter be able to add or to shed a sweater or jacket; you may well find offices that are cold to begin with become very stuffy and overheated later in the day.

It's a good idea to take along a little something to eat — an apple, perhaps, or a small bar of chocolate, or some crackers with a little piece of cheese. Exhaustion or nervousness may make you feel in need of a quick pick-me up. Also take a bottle of mineral water or fruit juice as you may find the machine-brewed coffee or tea available in most offices does not adequately quench your thirst.

Most women keep a kind of emergency drawer at work so that the unexpected does not catch them too much off guard. The contents might include tissues, a packet of tights, aspirin (or whatever you find beneficial in case of headache), plasters, tampons, comb, make-up, emery boards, travelling toothbrush and toothpaste, moisturiser, and perfume. If you varnish your nails, you must also keep by you nail varnish remover and a bottle of polish. (Nothing, but nothing, ruins a woman's professional appearance more that chipped nail polish or laddered tights.) In addition, keep handy some postcards and a couple of birthday cards, so that keeping up with your network of social contacts is possible. A travelling sewing kit is invaluable for catching up a hem that has become unravelled or sewing on a button. And it is useful to have handy something to spruce up your shoes.

On your first day, take along a trade magazine or a quality daily newspaper so that if you are left without anything to do at first, you won't look too much at a loss.

In a well-run organization some thought should have been given to your first day before you arrive. A desk should have been cleared for you to sit at and, unless there is some very good reason for it, it should be the desk you are going to occupy for the foreseeable future. Someone should make sure that you are introduced to your new colleagues, that you know the personnel officer and office manager and that you have a clear idea of who to turn to if you have problems with a machine or need to have some office procedure explained.

If your supervisor does not see to it that these introductions are made, *ask*. It is not easy to remember people's names at first, so ask for a telephone list so that you can tick off the people you have been introduced to and check how their names are spelt. If it is an open-plan office make a seating plan of the area and note on it people's names and positions. You may want to make a few notes, too, on what they do, their job title, and any special responsibilities they may have. Just doing this simple task will ensure that you quickly get to know your colleagues and can find your way around. You may not be given very much to do on the first day, but your supervisor should give you an idea of what he or she wants you to accomplish by the end of a certain period of time. Again, if you are in doubt about what is expected of you, *ask*.

One of the quickest ways to find out what is going on is to read through the correspondence files and to read any minutes or reports relevant to your projects. Time should be set aside for you to do this and if you feel that your supervisor has asked for you to do too much at once, say that you would welcome an orientation period in which to go through the files to build up a picture of the organization and its contacts, markets, support systems, and suppliers. An early grasp of this will give you a head start.

You must ask questions — lots of questions. You will find that it is easier to ask questions right at the beginning when no previous knowledge is assumed than later on when your colleagues will automatically assume that you know certain things. However, it is important that you don't play only the role of the learner in the first few days. At all costs avoid creating the impression that you are lost, out of your depth, dependent and helpless. When you ask for more information, it is because you are an adult in an adult situation and you want to control that situation. Your search for information is in recognition that knowledge is power. The more you know, the better you are oriented to the job, the more easily you can prove yourself master of the situation. This is important, for it is going to determine where you are going and how quickly you will get there.

Management for life

If you aspire to manage others, you must begin with yourself, and to do this you must know yourself, your strengths and your weaknesses. The assessment of yourself you used to form the basis of your c.v. will help you here. Keep it up to date at all times. To begin with, to go forward you must know what you want from life. You are having to juggle personal responsibilities and professional commitments. Often they conflict. You or your partner and family have to make sacrifices. It's tough and it's tiring. You must know how much it all matters to you. It is always a good idea to reflect on your personal and professional life and review your goals regularly to establish your priorities. See whether there is any room for manoeuvre in what you are doing now to enable you to develop — perhaps you feel you need more training for your work, perhaps you feel you would like more time for some creative activity at home. Extra time or free time has to be made somehow and for this you may need to negotiate with your boss or your partner.

Review your life and set your goals regularly, every six months or so, in order for you to evaluate progress. What you decided in January may not be compatible with the way events have moved on by June. Also you should ask yourself whether the way you are spending your life is right for you. It is easy for hectic days to rush past, every minute filled, and suddenly something you didn't really want to miss out on has indeed passed you by. Perhaps your partner dies or becomes incapacitated. Or perhaps you, rushing, rushing, always rushing, are yourself pulled up short by a physical breakdown.

You may find it helpful to ask yourself what you would like your family and friends to remember you for, what qualities would you feel most pleased to have had and what achievements would you like to feel proud of having accomplished. Will your children say what a wonderful career you had — pity you didn't have time for them? Will your friends say what a gift you had for music — pity you didn't enjoy it? Will your partner wonder about that special holiday to the Far East you'd promised each other? What about that book you were always going to write? It's a sad fact that it is often the very things we feel to be most important that we postpone. Inevitably life contains regrets, but we all have to try to live life in such a way that there aren't too many waiting for us in retirement and old age. To do that we need to manage our time.

To achieve goals we need to work at them regularly and systematically, a bit at a time. Once you know what your goals are, weigh and value them. Which ones matter to you most? Start with those and create an action plan for yourself. Make sure it is feasible. To do this you need to work out how much of your time you are able to control. Who else shares your time with you? Is this time you bestow willingly upon them or is it time that is demanded — perhaps for an extra meeting called by your boss the very evening you had arranged to go to a concert. What contingencies do you have for finding time for a close friend who needs to confide in you, or your devastated eighteen-year old who's just failed a driving test?

Using time well is a skill and one that can be learned and practised every day. First of all, find out — and be honest — how you spend your time. Do others usurp your time? Do you spend too much time deliberating and not enough time in action? Is

164

your feeling of not having enough time due to poor planning? Most important of all is to ask yourself continually whether the present task you are engaged upon is the best use of your time.

Strategies for time management

You've heard the expression, "Time is money". Time is also like money in that once you have spent it on one thing, you can't also have it to spend again on another. Like money, time is a valuable resource that must be invested in productive assets. Before committing time to a particular activity ask yourself what are the benefits likely to be and weigh them against the rest of your programme. Activities that are not likely to bear fruit should be dropped.

Given that the job is worth doing, are you the best person to do it. Can someone else do it? Developing your delegating skills is a crucial factor in moving up the career ladder; it is only by delegating that you will be able to release yourself for more valuable activities such as planning, policy making, developing new ideas and new markets. Ask yourself several times during the day "Is what I am doing now the best use of my time? Is there anyone else who could do the task instead?"

To ensure that you always make the best use of your time you must plan how you will use it — and then stick to that plan. One of the most exhausting and ineffectual things to be is someone who only responds to other people's demands. The key to effective time planning is the list. Every day, either first thing in the morning or, preferably, last thing in the evening, you should make a list of what you have to do or to delegate during the day ahead. Prioritize tasks — and then stick to your list, working steadily through the tasks you have set yourself. Any items not completed by the end of the day should be moved on to the list for the following day so that they are not forgotten. Only in this way will you be able to dominate and control your time.

Continue to set your sights

The most enjoyable jobs in any organization are near the top. They are more interesting, better rewarded, and offer more

165

satisfying challenges. There is also the question of power — always more fun to wield than to defer to. Successful people are happier and healthier than the unsuccessful. Moving up in an organization means you will mix with other successful people and have more stimulation and more fun. As you move on and upwards, however, the competition for jobs becomes ever more fierce. You will need to continue to practise your self-confidence building exercises and to keep up your c.v. up to date, constantly setting your sights on the next opportunity for promotion and growth. Let your employers know that you are ambitious and remember to dress for the job you aspire to rather than the job you already have. It will be easier to promote you to higher status if you look as though you already possess that higher status.

When the time comes for promotion you will probably have to face another interview. Again, you will have to to emphasize your strengths and skills. This is where you can score over other candidates by using your self-evaluation exercises. Keep your record of achievements up to date, reviewing them every month at least. Don't expect to remember all your triumphs when promotion beckons without keeping a record of what you have achieved. Is productivity up because of your efforts? Have sales figures climbed? Have you been able to cut costs, find elegant solutions to problems, improve morale, and contribute creatively to the company's success? Every time you have had a good idea taken up or have implemented a successful programme, make a note of it so that you will be able to draw up a neat summary sheet of your achievements to take with you to appraisal and promotion interviews. But remember that successful people learn more from their mistakes than from their triumphs. If you can demonstrate that you can learn and grow and find ways of overcoming your weaknesses you will also be demonstrating your intelligence and maturity. And you can set your sights on promotion with quiet confidence in your ability to win.